RAF FIGHTER PILOT

R A F
FIGHTER
PILOT

TIM LAMING

W H ALLEN

First published in Great Britain in 1991 by
W. H. Allen & Co Plc
338 Ladbroke Grove
London W10 5AH

British Library Cataloguing in Publication Data
Laming, Tim
    RAF fighter pilot.
    1. Great Britain. Royal Air Force. Air forces. Pilots
    I. Title
    358.4307

ISBN 1-85227-216-3

Set in Palatino by Input Typesetting Ltd, London
Printed in Great Britain by
Butler & Tanner Ltd, Frome and London

'The Royal Air Force must always be in the forefront of the defence of our country if we are ever again called upon to take up arms in the cause of liberty.'

HM QUEEN ELIZABETH II

CONTENTS

CONTENTS

ILLUSTRATIONS

PREFACE

The peace and tranquillity of an early morning in Suffolk is broken by the urgent sound of a warning horn and the rumble of two huge blast doors, which slowly open to reveal an expensive and deadly treasure. Inside a concrete, blast-proof shelter stands a multi-million-pound fighter aircraft; a Phantom, carrying four heat-seeking missiles and four radar-guided missiles, together with a fearsome-looking cannon, containing 1200 rounds of ammunition. The Phantom is an old aircraft, but it is also a machine which pilots both young and old treat with great respect. Unlike many modern warplanes, the Phantom proved its capabilities in wartime conflict, when the United States deployed hundreds of the type to Vietnam. As the pilots will testify, she's a 'mean machine'.

From a nearby office block, two people emerge into the sunlight, only to disappear quickly into an adjoining doorway, closing a huge steel door behind them. They have entered the PBF, the Personnel Briefing Facility, where the 'nerve-centre' of their RAF squadron is located. Inside the PBF they would be protected against nuclear attack, chemical attack and biological attack, sealed in their 'hardened' accommodation. On a bright morning in the heart of the English countryside, waging war might seem to be a strange pursuit, but the RAF, ever-present to defend the United Kingdom, takes its job seriously and, to be effective, the RAF has to be constantly prepared for the 'unthinkable'. Inside the PBF, the two-man crew of the Phantom dress for their day's work, equipping themselves for a flight which will be planned in minute detail, and they are briefed inside the same building, where three more Phantom crews prepare to discuss their four-aircraft mission.

An hour later, the door of the PBF is re-opened, and the crews walk to their aircraft, each machine housed in its own bomb-proof HAS (Hardened Aircraft Shelter). The navigator is first to climb the access ladder that reaches to the cockpits, and as he settles himself into the rear seat (which he wryly calls his 'office'), the pilot makes a thorough inspection of the aircraft, checking for any obvious faults which might make his job even more dangerous than it always is. The ground crew have already ensured that the aircraft is in good condition, but the pilot always takes a look for himself, prior to joining the navigator on board.

Once inside the cockpit, the crew must attach themselves to their seats; ejection seats, capable of firing them out of the aircraft and away from danger, to a parachute recovery. Only a life-or-death emergency would cause the crew to fire their escape system, as a rocket-powered departure is certainly no fun, and both the pilot and navigator strap themselves tightly to the seats; even a spare inch of slack in the harness could cause broken bones in an ejection. The safety pins are withdrawn from the seats, and they are then 'live', ready to be operated by the pull of a large black-and-yellow striped handle attached to the base of the seat.

Slowly the Phantom comes to life, and the crew make contact with each other through a radio channel. The conversation is complicated to the ears of an outsider, and muffled by the rubber oxygen masks that the crew wear. The ground crew are signalled by hand, and the two J-79 engines are started, the interior of the shelter rapidly filling with fumes, and noise. With the two perspex canopies closed, and their 'bonedome' safety helmets tightly fitted, only the RT chatter can be heard by the pilot and navigator. Ahead of them, three more F-4Js appear from within the complex of concrete and barbed wire, and together the aircraft weave their way towards the runway.

The first two aircraft rush down the runway and soar into the sky, as the second pair arrive at the runway threshold. There's no hurry to follow, as the lead aircraft are carrying external fuel tanks, and with an extra 'gas supply' they can afford to spend a little longer in the air. The second pair of Phantoms are being flown 'clean', with no fuel tanks hung under their wings. The smaller amount of fuel means a shorter flight, but the equally smaller amount of aerodynamic drag will increase the Phantom's already startling performance. 'She'll go like a bat out of hell.' And she does.

Lined up on the runway, and with clearance to take-off obtained from the control tower, the pilot pushes the two throttle levers forward as he signals to his 'playmate', just a few feet away to his right, to do the same. The combined power of the two engines running-up to full power makes the aircraft rumble and groan: the instruments start to shake visibly, and in his rear-view mirrors the navigator can see a cascade of brown smoke rising from behind the aircraft. With a decisive nod, the first pilot releases the wheel brakes, the second pilot follows, and the two aircraft jump into motion as the throttle levers are pushed still further forward into reheat position. With a surge of power and acceleration, the engine afterburners light up, and their plumes of flame send a spray of early-morning frost and water into the air from the runway surface. The Phantoms thunder down the runway, and in a matter of seconds the speed indicator tells the pilot that he has reached 80 knots, at which speed he is able to control the direction of the aircraft on the ground with his rudder, rather than by steering the wheels. At 140 knots he pulls back his control-column 'joystick' very slightly, and the nose of the aircraft begins to rise. At a speed of just under 200 mph, he pulls the control column back still further and the Phantom lifts gently into the air, with the second aircraft still beside him, bobbing up and down in the turbulence. It's taken less than twenty seconds from releasing the brakes to being airborne.

Once safely into the air, the extended wing flaps are retracted and the undercarriage is tucked away, the thud of the landing gear doors closing being felt by the navigator (the limiting speed at which the gear can be left extended is 250 knots, reached just seconds after take-off). Positioned in a gentle climb, the two fighters set course to a refuelling tanker aircraft which is waiting for them out over the North Sea.

Climbing through 20,000 feet, the crews of the four aircraft are in radio contact with each other, and a rendezvous is made alongside a Tristar tanker, where all four aircraft can refill their fuel tanks prior to beginning the real business of the day, a series of practice low-level intercepts over northern England. Each aircraft in turn slowly approaches the single refuelling 'basket' which is trailed behind the massive bulk of the Tristar — a converted Pan-Am airliner. From the right-hand side of the Phantom's fuselage a refuelling probe is extended, and with some careful positioning the probe is flown into the tanker's basket. The fuel then rapidly flows and in a few minutes the four-ship is ready to depart.

The high-level refuelling completed, they leave the cruising tanker in the safety of turbulence-free altitude, and descend to low-level, turning inland. Then, over the bleak snow-covered hills of the Lake District, the Phantom crews can initiate their first moves in a complicated world of 'yo-yo's', 'reversals', 'brackets' and other equally bewildering descriptions. The rules of this game are many and varied. They are also followed rigidly, as air-to-air combat is a deadly business which, even in peacetime, could have devastating consequences should it go wrong. The lives of the crews are at stake, the lives of people on the ground are at stake. The pilot has to be trained well in his trade. It might appear to be a game, but its purpose couldn't be more serious, and to sample a typical day's work first-hand is an astonishing experience.

At low level, the RAF imposes a minimum height limit of 250 feet. No RAF aircraft is permitted to fly below that height. There are also hundreds of avoidance areas, airways, restricted airspaces, and a variety of other pinpoints on the navigator's map, which have to be avoided. As the four-ship splits into pairs, the crews are busy not only avoiding towns, villages and much more, but also constantly checking height and steering clear of the surrounding terrain which rapidly rises and falls as the Phantoms sweep by at nearly 500 mph. The exercise begins, and the navigators endeavour to locate their 'playmates' on their radar screens, performing a series of low-level intercepts. At 250 feet it's difficult to find another fighter on radar, but that is the real reason for training at this height. Should an enemy bomber or fighter ever appear, he will be at low level, hiding his radar image in the 'clutter' at low level. Naturally it makes sense to train in the same environment, and the RAF would like to fly much lower, maybe down to just 50 feet at times. But with due regard to both safety and the goodwill of the general public, the 250-feet rule is strictly enforced.

No sooner has the exercise begun, than the Phantoms are spotted on the radar screens of some other RAF fighters which are in the same area. The Tornado F3s join in, and the result is a mind-blowing 'fight', with Phantom against Phantom, and Tornado against Phantom, the pilots hauling the aircraft around to position themselves to 'get a kill'. Not that anyone is planning to shoot anyone else down. The exercise is simulated, but the effect is very real; and learning to fly a fighter as a fighter, and not just a useless aeroplane, is a complex business. Inside the Phantom, the world is rolling from side to side turning over altogether: and everything is rattling and shaking, the hillsides rolling by at what would seem to an untrained observer to be a distance of only a few inches at times. With every turn a g-force comes into effect, the centrifugal-force effect pushing the crew tightly down into their seats, in a face-pulling, gut-wrenching turn through what appears to be a hopelessly narrow valley. With another agonising pull of 5g (five times the normal force of gravity, and that's a fairly gentle manoeuvre by modern standards), the Phantom shoots upwards and out from the valley, rolling over on its back and down the hillside into another 'hiding place'. Another 'enemy' Phantom flashes into view heading straight towards the nose, with a halo of water vapour surrounding its unmistakable front profile. It rushes by beneath the wings, turning hard to close in for a tail-chase, a perfect missile-firing position. It can be difficult even to remain conscious if the manoeuvres become too hard, but the pilots are used to the conditions and, as they are controlling the moves, they know what to expect. The navigator, working hard with his radar, not only has to look for 'targets' on his screen but has to hang on for the ride, too. It's little wonder that many navigators are regularly airsick.

The fight seems to last forever, but in reality there are only a few minutes of fuel-burning combat before it's time to 'knock it off' and head for home. Back over the airfield, the aircraft join the airfield circuit, and circle the runway for individual landings. With the speed back down to a 'sedate' 200 mph, the landing gear and flaps are extended, and with continual bursts of power from the engines, each Phantom is guided round the airfield traffic pattern, and down with a firm bump on to the runway, before streaming a braking parachute.

Once back on the ground, the Phantoms are prepared for the next mission, and the aircrew return to the PBF to debrief, discussing what went right and what went wrong, sharing their views and experiences in preparation for the next exercise. Their next mission may be days away, or it could be just a couple of hours away; sometimes three sorties can be flown in one day. The training never ends, even for a fully-qualified front-line fighter pilot. There is always something new to learn in the world of aerial combat. It's a complicated and incredibly demanding job. It requires many years of teaching, training and experience. It costs the taxpayer a huge amount of money. It also provides the United Kingdom with a defence capability that is second to none.

The following pages represent a personal look at life in today's Royal Air Force. Through a series of visits to a variety of RAF units, I was able, over the space of more than a year, to obtain a glimpse of how the RAF selects and trains its force of 'fast-jet' pilots. I use the term 'fast-jet' in deference to RAF terminology, but the phrase hardly does full justice to the realities of life as a pilot of a modern high-performance jet fighter-bomber. Racing over a bleak hillside at a height of just 250 feet, at a speed of 500 mph, brings a whole new meaning to the term 'fast'. RAF pilots fly in this kind of environment every day, as part of a normal training mission.

The reason why the RAF trains so hard became evident in January 1991, when the RAF went to war, and put years of hard training into practice, flying continual attacks against targets in Iraq and occupied Kuwait. Hitting targets that were heavily defended required skill, professionalism and an incredible amount of courage. Despite daily casualties, the RAF crews pressed home their devastating attacks, flying at phenomenal speed, day and night, good weather and bad, at heights of less than fifty feet above the unfriendly desert sands. High in the sky, the fighter elements hunted Saddam Hussein's air force, destroying Iraqi fighters as they climbed into battle. Many enemy pilots didn't even hang around to test their skill or their nerve; they dashed for safety once the RAF fighters locked their radars on to them.

Since I first made my visits to RAF units around Europe, much has taken place which will directly affect the future status and composition of the Royal Air Force. Naturally, in a book of this nature, it's impossible to offer a completely up-to-date picture of RAF life, as circumstances change continually, and the RAF has to adapt to reflect the needs of the United Kingdom. The arrival, and partial subsequent departure, of glasnost in the Soviet Union encouraged Nato to move towards large-scale conventional and nuclear disarmament, tempered by the later troubles which plagued Gorbachev's premiership. The outbreak of a full-scale war in the Gulf served to illustrate how unforeseen events can quickly develop into a huge requirement for airpower. The future of the Gulf region will, whatever occurs, require the widespread presence of military aircraft.

However, some changes have already been made, or have been announced, which are relevant to the information contained in the following pages. The Officer and Aircrew Selection Centre at Biggin Hill is to close in 1992, and the OASC will move to RAF Cranwell in Lincolnshire. Thus the famous Battle of Britain fighter station in Kent will no longer be an RAF station. The station chapel and the Spitfire and Hurricane 'guards' will remain, as a tribute to those who flew their combat sorties from Biggin Hill in 1940. The faithful Jet Provost continues its slow disappearance from the RAF training units, and the new Shorts Tucano is gradually becoming a more familiar sight, training more and more student pilots, although the training courses have remained essentially unchanged. The Panavia Tornado GR1 will replace Buccaneers in the maritime strike role, and will replace remaining Jaguars in the reconnaissance role. The Tornado F3 will soon assume the duties of the remaining Phantom air defence squadrons, and, as an indication of things to come, the F-4Js belonging to 74 Squadron (as featured in the penultimate chapter), have already been retired from service. RAF Wildenrath in Germany will close, its Phantoms being retired, and a Tornado F3 unit will assume air defence duties in Germany, at Laarbruch. RAF Gutersloh will also close, the Harriers returning to the UK.

Whilst equipment changes continue, the training and day-to-day life has not altered. If the destructive power of Operation Desert Storm has had any direct effect upon the RAF, it has been the sudden public realisation that the service does, despite the end of the Cold War, have a vitally important purpose. The need for effective airpower has been fiercely demonstrated in the sands of Iraq and Kuwait.

To examine every aspect of RAF operations in detail, I would need many years, and a series of books. In this particular publication, I have confined my efforts to an honest look at just one area, that of the high-performance jet pilot. But having concentrated my interest on just one specific area of RAF operations, I hope I can give a fair indication of what RAF life is like, and something of what it takes to become a fast-jet pilot in today's Royal Air Force.

ACKNOWLEDGEMENTS

Many years have passed since I first decided to write a book about the RAF. I visited many RAF stations and spoke to countless numbers of RAF personnel, and without exception, every individual happily gave freely of their time to answer questions. In some instances I was fortunate to be given an opportunity to try some exercises and some flying 'firsthand'; and to all those who guided this particular inexperienced civilian through the complex world of the military, I must express my gratitude. Whilst it would be practically impossible to name everyone who assisted me with this project, I must record a few thank-you's to the following: OASC Biggin Hill, AMTC North Luffenham, EFTS Swiderby, DIOT Cranwell, 1 FTS Linton-on-Ouse, 7 FTS Church Fenton, 4 FTS Valley, CFS Scampton, 1 Group Upavon, No. 19 Squadron, No. 63 Squadron, No. 74 Squadron, No. 101 Squadron, No. 111 Squadron, No. 208 Squadron, No. 229 OCU, and the CROs at Coningsby, Wittering, Cottesmore, Brawdy, Chivenor, Lossiemouth, Brize Norton, Leuchars, Wattisham, Marham, Valley, Scampton, and Public Information, British Forces Germany. Finally my special thanks to the Public Relations Office, Support Command and Michael Hill CPRO Strike Command, for their tremendous support and seemingly endless amounts of patience, for which I am most grateful.

Tim Laming

1

A LITTLE APPLICATION

'The name of Biggin Hill is famous in British history. Today, of course, the operational aircraft have long since departed, but as the home of the Officers and Aircrew Selection Centre, its role is still important to the RAF — and to the nation.' This written introduction is given to every young man who applies to join the Royal Air Force as a fast-jet pilot, prior to attending the OASC. Every RAF pilot's career begins at Biggin Hill, no matter what his background or circumstances, as this single establishment is responsible for the selection of all RAF aircrew and officers. If OASC accepts the applicant, he can go on to be trained as an officer, and ultimately a pilot. If he is rejected, he can't; it's as simple as that.

'Our standards are high and we apply them strictly. We make no apology for that. We are in the business of selecting the next generation of officers for a high technology fighting service, ready to defend Britain in the

event of war. The men and women we select will be
given a long and expensive training, leading to a very
demanding job; they are likely to be responsible not only
for millions of pounds' worth of sophisticated equipment,
but for the wellbeing — maybe the lives — of others.
Wrong choices on our part would be costly in more ways
than one, and we cannot take chances.'

Providing the entry qualifications are met, virtually
everyone is given an opportunity to attend OASC: 'We
send them to Biggin Hill to prove themselves . . . it's up
to them to show us what they're made of.'

RAF pilots are all commissioned officers; there are no
non-commissioned officer (NCO) pilots, and it can be
something of a surprise to the uninitiated that the RAF
insists that all would-be pilots are trained as RAF officers
first, before flying training is commenced.

The applicants arrive at OASC in groups of between 30
and 40 — some in cars, the majority from nearby Bromley
railway station. After reporting to the guardroom, they
are directed to their accommodation to deposit their lug-
gage, prior to reporting to the OASC Headquarters
Building.

Giving applicants a taste of things to come is very
much part of the OASC philosophy, and, over a three-
day period, the group of candidates will be tested both
physically and mentally. They will be expected to cope
with all manner of situations, and although the OASC
staff are keen to relax the candidates, the capacity to cope
with pressure is a prerequisite for any RAF pilot, and it
is a quality that Biggin Hill will look for in great detail.

Inside the headquarters building, the duty officer wel-
comes the candidates to OASC and explains the variety
of events that will be taking place over the next couple
of days. The comfortable surroundings of the reception
lounge will serve as a central base for the candidates,
from where they will be sent to their tests, examinations
and exercises. There is always a good supply of magazines to hand, and a range of RAF video films, but no
matter how many distractions are made available, the
occupants of the reception lounge never have any desire

to relax — the constant fear of failure is too strong for that.

'It is no part of our policy to try and make you nervous or catch you with trick questions. The interviews and tests are carried out in a relaxed and informal way. We need to get to know you as a person as well as we can in the time available, and we can only hope to do this if we encourage you to feel at home and to think and act naturally. In fact, most candidates will enjoy their time at Biggin Hill. If you come here in the right spirit we believe that you will too. And whether or not you are successful, you should learn something about today's RAF and the people in it — and about yourself.'

Certainly there is no sense of competition between the candidates; if they all meet the OASC's standards they are all accepted for training. On the other hand, if they fail to meet the required standards they can all be rejected too, and it is with this knowledge that each candidate comes to Biggin Hill. The OASC has a reputation for toughness, but few applicants are deterred from their ambition and determination to become RAF pilots. Many have wanted nothing else all their lives, and have simply been waiting until they had the required qualifications to attend: 'I've never been interested in any other job, I just want to be up there in a Tornado racing down a valley.'

Some have a more practical outlook: 'Well, I don't want to sit in an office all my life. I want to do something with a bit of excitement. I want to learn some new skills.' After the initial introductions, the first evening is normally spent in the Candidate's Club, where the new arrivals get to know each other, and discuss their mutual interests. It is surprising to see how wide the background of the people who attend OASC really is. The image of the 'typical public-school type' still persists in civilian life, but even the most cursory glance at the candidates' background details will reveal that today's prospective RAF aircrew come from each and every section of British life. Indeed, the only quality they seem to share is the same ambition — to fly. Quite how strong their desire really is, will be revealed over the following days.

In the relaxed atmosphere of the Candidates' Club, complete with TV rooms, games rooms and a bar, the comments flow: 'I saw all the adverts, and I thought I'd have a go.' 'I've always rather fancied the idea.' 'I've heard lots of stories about how difficult getting through Biggin Hill can be.' The most apprehensive of all the candidates must be the 'Hairies' — the serving NCO airmen who have decided to apply to become commissioned officers and pilots. Not only do they have a much clearer idea of what RAF life is really like; they have also endured endless horror stories (mostly untrue) from their colleagues about the rigours of Biggin Hill and officer training. They also know that they will have to face the possibility of rejection, in which case they will have to return to their previous duties as airmen — an ideal situation for no end of leg-pulling.

The next day begins at 06:30, and after breakfast Part One of the selection procedure begins: the four and a half hour aptitude test. The series of individual tests has recently entered the computer age, and the days of paper exercises and Heath Robinson-style machines are almost gone. The candidates sit in their own cubicles, facing a television screen and a keyboard, and after an introduction by the supervising officer, the tests begin. Each one is designed to explore a specific skill related to flying: 'If you are a candidate for pilot or navigator, you will take a series of specialised tests designed to measure your chances of success in flying training. These range from multiple-choice written exercises, to machine or computer-generated tests, and can take up to six hours in all. They show your ability to deal accurately and at high speed with mathematical, scientific and mechanical problems. The computerised tests assess your speed of reaction, your natural sense of timing, your co-ordination of hands, eyes and feet, and your ability to handle constantly changing information.' The tests sound like a frightful ordeal, and to some they are: 'There's one where you get a series of numbers . . . I think it's four, and you have to memorise them and type them on to the screen. Then you get five numbers, then six and so on. I think it went to about twelve before it finished . . . I couldn't remember them all.'

The aptitude tests are not subjective. Because it is essentially a computer-orientated examination, the results are compiled in numerical form, and the candidate will simply be judged against a pre-determined target total. Thus it cannot be anything but fair, even if it is a most frustrating experience. 'They give you an outline of an aircraft, placed in lots of different positions, and you have to say which direction you think it's travelling . . . they give you a list to choose from . . . there's one with a layout like an instrument panel where you have to decide what the aircraft would be doing, judging by the instrument positions.' Some of the tests are more challenging than others: 'The one with a little circle on a horizontal line is a killer . . . well, the circle keeps moving left and right, and you have to key in the corrections to keep it central . . . at the same time a square will light up on the screen, which you are asked to cancel, but the only way to do it is by getting the circle central first, so you have to cope with two problems at once.'

Perhaps the biggest handful is the Sensory Motor Application test. This consists of a dot placed centrally on the TV screen, within a small reference frame, which can be moved to the left and right through the operation of two foot pedals. The vertical motion is controlled by a small joystick, and the task is apparently quite simple — to keep the dot in the centre of the small frame. It sounds easy, and when the tests begin it proves to be so, with just small hand and foot movements being sufficient to nudge the dot back into position. Of course things soon get a little more complicated, and the dot begins to move off completely at random around the screen. The candidate's natural instinct is to try and correct either the vertical or horizontal movement, but not both at once. In order to cope effectively with the exercise, the candidates quickly have to learn the skill of controlling their hands and feet simultaneously in response to the image presented on the screen, and the gasps of frustration in the adjoining cubicles only serve to confirm that everyone finds the test a real challenge.

Many of the aptitude tests bear a resemblance to a 'Space Invaders' game ('we find that the candidates can relate to this sort of thing'), but the demanding nature of these 'games' allows OASC to sift out those who cannot cope with large inputs of information, and those who simply lack the necessary hand, foot and eye co-ordination which is essential in the fast-jet environment. 'A pilot's got to be able to fly the machine without thinking too much about it, so that he can concentrate on other things, especially the weaponry he is likely to be carrying.'

Anyone who fails to meet the required standard in the aptitude tests will be reviewed by a member of the OASC staff, and advised of his failure. If the candidate so desires, he can be placed back into the selection procedure for training within another RAF specialisation (there is a Careers Advice Bureau in the headquarters building). On the other hand, if the candidate only wishes to be considered as a potential pilot, he will immediately be free to leave Biggin Hill. Reactions to failure are varied; some simply take a philosophical view and go off to pursue other careers. There are those however, who have to come to terms with a life's ambition suddenly being shattered — tears are not uncommon.

The medical examination is another objective phase, in that those who don't meet the set standards will be rejected. Many of the candidates are somewhat surprised to find that so much attention is paid to medical condition: 'I began to wonder what it was all about . . . what am I letting myself in for here?' The examination includes thorough eyesight and hearing testing, and particular emphasis is placed on respiratory matters, especially the nasal passages. OASC is infamous for rejecting candidates with crooked noses (although an invitation is normally given to return after corrective surgery). And this is simply because aircrew must have clear air passages: 'Things can become difficult in ascent or descent if air cannot pass easily through the nasal passages. Particularly during a rapid descent, the pressure build-up could cause a perforated ear drum.' The candidates treat the medicals with good humour: 'There's things like blood pressure and blood sugar, reflexes, eyesight, hearing and things . . . It's quite a laugh . . . Standing on one leg with your eyes closed is quite good, it's harder than it sounds . . . Nobody was really worried, because you can't do anything to change things, you just have to wait and see . . . Then they ask for a sample, and we'd nearly all been to the toilet before we went in!'

Vital statistics are also noted in detail; not to establish uniform sizes, but to determine whether the candidate will physically fit into the confines of a fast-jet's cockpit. Such measurements really can be critical, when one considers the cramped conditions inside many front-line aircraft. Although most people might be able to sit in most cockpits, it is vitally important that one's limbs are not too short to reach the more remote switches, when strapped tightly to an ejection seat. ('It's like being trussed-up like a chicken.') Conversely, legs mustn't be too long, or they could come into contact with the cockpit instrument-panel coaming during an ejection, resulting in some very severe injuries. ('You could leave your knee-caps behind quite easily.') Physically speaking, OASC is looking for the elusive 'Mr Average'.

The next morning starts at 06:30 once more, and each candidate is sent in turn for an interview with two OASC Boarding Officers: 'You will be seen by a wing commander and a squadron leader who will talk to you on a friendly basis for forty minutes or thereabouts. During the interview they will invite you to talk about your family background, academic achievement, why you want to join the RAF, any previous experience you may have had in the Air Training Corps, the CCF or a University Air Squadron, and any positions of responsibility you may have held at school or university, or in voluntary organisations such as the Scouts or Guides. They will also want to find out whether you take an interest in current affairs. This interview is independent of the aptitude tests — the Boarding Officers will not have seen the results of these.

Their job is to find out whether you possess — in embryo at least — the qualities the RAF is looking for in its officers. 'The best advice we can give you is to be yourself. Tell the Boarding Officers what you honestly believe, and not what you think they might want to hear. If you do not meet our standards, you will be withdrawn from the testing at this stage.'

Each officer conducts half of the interview, while the other officer completes an interview report, noting factual information given by the candidate, and also writing down observational points on the candidate's personal background, academic background, awareness and motivation. During the first half of the interview, the candidate will be guided through his life, from birth to the present day, covering family background, schooling, interests, employment and so on, forming a fairly detailed chronological history of his social and academic background. Although much of the interview is conducted on an informal basis, some questions are framed more formally: 'What trouble, if any, have you had with the police?' 'What will you do in the event of this application being unsuccessful?' and 'Have you had any involvement with drugs?'

The candidate's answers are noted in full, and the interview is completed, the candidate returning — with some relief — to the reception lounge, while the two Boarding Officers spend another ten minutes discussing their assessment, prior to agreeing on a grading figure: 'I thought this guy was a real Mr Average, you know, but I think the potential is there . . . Now this chap was a typical country lad. He's never been away from home, doesn't know much about anything really, but he's very enthusiastic . . . ' Those that manage to satisfy the officers that they do at least have the potential for further examination are syndicated for the afternoon exercise phase, whilst those that fail the interview are informed of the Boarding Officers' decision and are released from the OASC. There is a small crumb of comfort for those that are released at this stage, in that they do at least have the knowledge that they have negotiated both the aptitude and medical tests successfully, and (providing they don't exceed the age limit) are free to return to OASC at a later date. 'They said that I was free to come back if I wished, but they wouldn't say why I'd failed the interview, which I thought was a bit off. If they told you, then maybe you could do something about it, whereas if I come back again I might be simply wasting another four days of holiday leave from my job. Anyway, I did enjoy the time I was there . . . yes, I did learn quite a bit about myself too . . . and I will go back and give it another try.'

The Boarding Officers have a difficult job in deciding whether a candidate should go through to the Part Two tests, because the interview is essentially a subjective examination, and it's easy to form the wrong opinion of someone in the short time available. On the other hand, the officers have seen so many different applicants, they do have an uncanny ability to sift out the sort of person they're looking for: 'We don't profess to be perfect, but we're as good as we can be, and we like to think that we'd give someone the benefit of the doubt if he's a bit borderline. We're very thorough, and we probably know more about him than he does himself by the time we're finished with him. We do not try to form an opinion too quickly, as it's so easy to pick up on the wrong aspects of someone's character . . . I think we're pretty fair on the whole.'

The Part Two exercises begin the same afternoon, in one of the old airfield hangars, where the candidates assemble after having dressed in grey overalls, each with an identifying code number. The numbers don't have any significance and are used simply as a means of identification. The reason why the candidates are dressed in overalls is twofold. Firstly there's an obvious need to wear clothing that is more suited to the physical activities performed in the hangar, but also the candidates will now be assessed as part of a group of five or six people, and a grey uniform ensures that nobody sticks out from the crowd. 'We find that the grey overalls help everyone to settle down together — it's a great leveller.'

9

After having a group photograph taken (again for identification) the Leaderless exercise begins on one of a range of obstacle courses arranged inside the hangar. Each course is different, but generally makes use of standard items of equipment such as ropes, tyres, oil drums, wooden beams and wooden planks. Areas are divided up into white and black sections, and each syndicate of half-a-dozen candidates is simply required to work through the course within a set time period, without coming into contact with any of the black sections. Of course the tests are slightly more cunning than they might at first appear, in that the wooden planks or ropes are generally a couple of inches too short to fulfil any useful purpose in isolation, and the candidates will have to apply some constructive (and rather lateral) thinking to the situation in order to get each person from the start to the end of the course.

In fact, the successful completion of the course isn't particularly important to the Boarding Officers, as they are really using the exercise as a forum in which each candidate can demonstrate how he works within a group. There are no appointed leaders to this exercise (as its name suggests), so the pressure to find a solution is spread evenly throughout the group, offering an ideal opportunity for the more assertive members to 'shine through'. However, this first hangar exercise is very much a 'settling-down' period, in which the candidates become familiar with the attitudes and capabilities of the other members of their syndicate.

In a nearby classroom, the Discussion Group exercise begins later in the afternoon: 'You will return to your syndicate room for an informal discussion on matters of current interest. The Boarding Officers will introduce and change the topics, but otherwise they stay out of the discussion. You will not be expected to produce off-the-cuff solutions to long-standing social problems, but we are interested in your ideas, and in hearing how well you express yourself.' The subject under discussion is irrelevant and frequently changed for a fresh topic as soon as the chatter appears to be in danger of drying up.

The Boarding Officers are again on the hunt for special qualities, in particular the powers of expression, initiative, influence and lucidity. Throughout the Part Two exercises, the two Boarding Officers will not be alone in their assessment role, as they now have an additional assessor in the shape of the Board President. He will oversee up to three syndicates simultaneously, by rapidly moving between groups, or by watching the overall scene through a network of closed-circuit TV cameras.

The final test for the day is the Planning exercise. 'This is a classroom exercise in which the syndicate is given a hypothetical situation to resolve. The problem calls for a team plan produced from syndicate discussion, after studying the situation brief. The syndicate will be questioned on the team plan by the Boarding Officers, and finally you will be asked to write a short essay outlining the team's plan.' The situations vary, but they all share the same qualities; for example, a team of jungle explorers, tasked with the transportation of natives from one location to another, taking into account the various rudimentary modes of transport available, an approaching forest fire, illnesses, and a variety of jungle tracks and river courses. The problem is generally one which requires much thought, and a capability to work out priorities, together with a good grasp of arithmetic. Working as a group, the syndicate will normally reveal those with particularly good powers of initiative and perception, and also those who are sufficiently forceful to persuade the group to adopt their way of thinking. Likewise, the candidates who are content to sit back and agree to everyone else's plans soon become obvious. The written description is also a valuable tool in establishing how capable the candidate may be at expressing himself in writing — a skill that many, perhaps rather surprisingly, don't possess. To OASC it is an important capability, as an officer who can't state matters clearly on a piece of paper isn't going to be of much use to the RAF. Once the group has defined a solution to the problem, the Boarding Officers fire searching questions at each candidate in turn. The pressure is on everyone to give the right answer, but sometimes, understandably enough, it just doesn't come. With this test complete, the day is over, and while the officers discuss their assessments from the exercises, the candidates return to the more comfortable environment of the Candidates' Club.

The final day encompasses the Confirmatory Phase, starting with the Individual Problem: 'In this exercise you work independently. Each of you is given a written brief describing some hypothetical situation for which you have to produce a solution, generally involving some arithmetic, reasoning and attention to detail. You present your solution orally to one of the Boarding Officers, and you will be questioned on it.' Again, the nature of the exercises changes between syndicates (but not within), although the basic task remains the same, no matter what the scenario. For example, you are to meet a group of friends at a motorway service station a specific number of miles away, at a specific time. You have to take some camping equipment, some of which you have to collect from a friend's house, and some which you will have to buy. The friend's house and the shop are all at specific distances from your home, and there are various routes which can be taken. However, there is only one bus connection, and the use of a bicycle (which, conveniently for the examiners, is not at your house), but your brother could give you a lift on his way to work at a specific time. The facts and figures are all there, and you have to get to the service station at the right time, or earlier. How do you do it? There appear to be a number of ways in which to solve the problem, but as the candidates set to work individually, with paper and pencil, they quickly realise that things are not so simple. In fact there is only one really effective solution to each problem, but it is up to each candidate to find it. After a study period, each candidate is interviewed privately by the Boarding Officers on his solution to the problem. He can use his written notes for answers, but the officers always manage to fire the odd question that catches the candidate out. The art of the exercise, as far as the assessors are concerned, is to apply pressure, to see how the candidate reacts. Will he give the right answers under pressure? Does he know what the right answers are? The interviewers never go so far as totally to confuse the candidates — just far enough to test the powers of arithmetic, comprehension, judgement and perception 'under fire'. Working under stress is the kind of environment that a fast-jet pilot is likely to become very familiar with, and OASC actively looks for those who have the type of character that can cope with such situations.

The final exercise is performed back in the hangar, on the obstacle course: 'You will each take turns in leading the syndicate through a different practical exercise. You are shown the particular task, given a short time to think out a plan, then, after briefing the team, you lead it through the exercise. It will help if you get yourself as fit as you can before coming to Biggin Hill. The exercises are not unduly strenuous, but they can take their toll if you are out of condition and, if your physical and mental energy start to flag, you may not do yourself justice.' Called the Command Situation, this final test is perhaps the most demanding for each individual. The chosen candidate is briefed on the task, while the other team members are tucked away in a nearby 'hide'. Once the candidate has studied the situation and worked out a plan, he calls in the other team members, and briefs them on his decision. Then the exercise begins, on yet another obstacle course. Although the Boarding Officers are still observing every candidate, they will be particularly interested in the individual who is leading the exercise, chiefly to establish whether he is doing just that. As in the earlier Leaderless exercise, the candidates are soon perched on high beams, swinging from ropes, and falling back into the black, out-of-bounds areas. 'Out number two, back one position . . . come on, twenty seconds to go, quickly, make an effort, go!' The officers prowl around the course, writing on to their clipboards, checking their stop-watches, watching for stray hands and feet falling into black areas. One officer watches as a candidate moves perilously close to an area designated as a minefield. He quietly lifts an oil drum from the floor. He

13

whispers, 'Watch this now — he's going to touch . . . '
With a great bang he slams the drum on to the floor as
an unwary foot touches the black area. 'Gets 'em every
time,' he comments with delight.

Each candidate takes a turn at leading an exercise, each
on a different course. The pressure is high; not only does
the candidate have to work out a successful course of
action, but he has to get himself and all the other team
members through the course within a time limit. It's the
assessors' last chance to confirm their views on each candidate, looking for the skills of leadership, and the ability
to motivate the other team members.

When each candidate has completed his individual
obstacle course, the tests are complete, and all that is left
is a final interview, in which a few minor administrative
details are cleared up, and the candidate is given an
opportunity to ask any questions he might have. Few
want to know anything other than when they will be told
the results of their stay at Biggin Hill, but the Boarding
Officers are not able to confirm or deny whether any
candidate has been successful. 'We will write and tell you
whether you have passed, normally in about three to four
weeks — Service candidates will be told through their
station commander. If four weeks seems a long time,
remember we have about eight thousand candidates a
year passing through Biggin Hill, and that each application has to be individually processed.'

Once the interview is over, the Boarding Officers
decide upon their grade for each candidate's performance
in the Part Two exercises: 'This guy is quite sound, and
I'm happy to accept this one . . . now this chap was a
really morose so-and-so, wasn't he? His attitude was starting to affect the rest of the syndicate at the end, I
thought . . . That one was a real old woman . . . Him?
Yes, he had some sparkle I felt, and he had some sparks
of initiative there . . . ' Eventually the Boarding Officers
and the Board President will get together, and a final
board grade will be aimed at for each candidate, taking
into account the results of each interview and exercise.
The candidate's likely results at officer training and flying

training are also considered, as well as the prevailing requirements for specific types of aircrew. 'Our aim is to eliminate those who are an unacceptable training risk, and to find those with a latent ability to develop a high-performance skill.'

The final word on selection is clear enough: 'As an OASC candidate, you will have realised by now that the tests are designed to reveal a wide spectrum of personal qualities, and you may be wondering whether some of them are really relevant to an RAF career. But the fact is that as an RAF officer you must play many parts. On the purely professional level, you must obviously have the mental and physical aptitudes for the branch you have chosen. On the wider view, you must be capable of leading a team and, at the same time, be prepared to take your place as a member of a larger team. You must be capable of showing firmness with consideration for others — leadership is not just ordering people about. You will have to stand up to stress; it is part of life in any fighting service. You will need a good grasp of current affairs — many RAF officers have to deal with members of the public in sensitive situations at home or overseas, and background knowledge and sympathetic understanding is essential. If this sounds like a demanding list, remember you are applying for a demanding job. That is why we have high standards and are tough in applying them. We have to be.'

2

AN OFFICER AND A GENTLEMAN

Those that have been accepted for further training are instructed to report to the DIOT (Department of Initial Officer Training) at RAF Cranwell in Lincolnshire. (Cranwell will also be the home of the OASC, following Biggin Hill's impending closure as an RAF station.) The DIOT is responsible for the training of every prospective RAF pilot, and aims to give the new arrivals a basic introduction to their chosen career as an RAF officer. To be more precise, the DIOT's aims are to provide entrants with general service and character training to enable them, after specialist training, to fill junior officer posts successfully, as well as to provide a basis from which their powers and faculties can eventually be developed to meet the demands of the highest ranks.

These aims are not new; they reflect policy laid down by Lord Trenchard when he set up the RAF College at Cranwell and, despite the changing of equipment and

17

responsibilities, the basic requirements that each officer must meet have remained the same. The RAF officer is expected to be able to command, lead and manage, in society, on the station and in ground defence duties. To this end, Cranwell aims to provide sufficient instruction to allow every officer cadet to 'find his or her way in the service'. The capacity to lead others, and to be able to manage situations and communicate, is considered vital. For the new officer cadets, their eighteen-week stay at Cranwell is generally regarded with mixed feelings. For many, it comes as something of a surprise to find that learning to fly an aeroplane is not their first preoccupation after joining the Service. Indeed, the world of aviation seems distinctly remote to the raw recruits, who quickly learn that the RAF regards all aviators as officers first, and pilots second. There are no short cuts to the flying training schools; if the cadets do not successfully complete their IOT course at Cranwell, they simply will not be allowed to train as pilots.

The DIOT is divided into five training squadrons: A, B, C, D and R (recourse), and each squadron in turn is sub-divided into up to fifteen flights consisting of between nine and eleven students. The flights are deliberately made up of cadets from widely differing backgrounds, such as serving airmen, university graduates, direct entrants from Biggin Hill, and Commonwealth students, as well as a proportion of WRAF cadets. The flights are not normally divided according to the cadet's chosen specialisation, the training being the same for every cadet. The Flight Commanders play an important part in the life of each cadet, spending a great deal of time in the company of their charges: 'Much of the cadet's inculcation of service standards, behaviour and values, is effected through the example of their Flight Commanders.'

Eight courses are run per year, with a maximum of 150 cadets per course. The overall success rate is 86 per cent, which reflects the fact that most cadets do eventually graduate from Cranwell. It would be wrong however, to imply that the IOT course is in any way 'easy', because this is far from the case: 'We get some people who think that getting through Cranwell will be a breeze . . . As they quickly find out, it's not that simple.' Week One begins with the traditional visit to the station barber; fortunately for the cadets, service-style 'short back and sides' are fashionable once more. Their civilian clothes are exchanged for military uniform, in both formal 'blues' and combat styles: 'The first week is really to sort out all the basics, like uniform and haircuts, form-filling and so on . . . it's a busy time for the cadets.' As the weeks progress, the General Service Training (GST) is introduced, dealing with a variety of subjects such as arms, leadership theory, etc.

Almost a quarter of the training syllabus is devoted to the art of written and oral communications, teaching the students to appreciate the various skills needed. Much of the teaching is performed in a practical fashion, for instance by giving each cadet an opportunity to give talks for specific time periods, or to conduct interviews. The talks are given to fellow cadets and the Flight Commander in a classroom equipped with closed-circuit television. It is up to the cadet to pick a suitable subject, and the choice is always a source of interest, if not amusement. From the relatively straightforward 'functions of an SLR camera', to 'the history of the haggis', the subject isn't really important, as it's the way in which the cadet presents it to the audience which counts. While the cadets are invited to look for constructive criticism, the Flight Commander makes a more detailed appraisal, noting precise detail on the cadet's confidence, enthusiasm, audibility, enunciation, pace, mannerisms, eye contact, and much more. The use of VAs (visual aids) is encouraged, and the way in which the cadet uses such 'props' is also noted. The extent to which the subject has been researched; how the talk is structured; overall delivery and impact; all are scrutinised in detail. It's quite an ordeal, and the 'debriefing' isn't much fun either, as the TV recording is replayed and discussed. The cadets generally cringe and sink into their seats and yet, rather perversely, they enjoy the experience — in retrospect.

Still with the world of communications, the Office

Simulator is another practical exercise, giving the cadets first-hand experience of life in a typical administrative position on an RAF station. Playing the roles of station executives is a useful way of demonstrating the responsibilities of different positions, and although the office exercises are set within artificial situations devised by the DIOT staff, the appropriate actions are quickly learned by the cadets. Some of the scenes contain plenty of scope for decision-making, such as an 'angry farmer' complaining about low-flying aircraft, or the NCO who has damaged a vehicle. The key parts are played by cadets, while staff officers generally portray the 'supporting cast' with varying degrees of tongue-in-cheek humour. The whole exercise is performed in a very light-hearted manner, and is treated as a 'bit of a laugh' by cadets and instructors alike. The serious purpose remains, however, and the informal approach pays off in results.

If the Office Simulator is something of an amusement, ceremonial drill is quite the opposite. Conducted under the watchful eye of a senior NCO, the frosty mornings on the parade square have changed little since the days of national service, and 'square-bashing' is as unpopular as it ever was. It has an important function of course, in teaching self-discipline and creation of team spirit, and the cadets admit that drill does encourage them to take pride in their personal appearance and performance. The many hours spent on the drill square do have their more uplifting moments, however: as Cranwell is also the home of a Tucano squadron, the skies are continually occupied with passing aircraft, and the aspiring pilots always 'get a boost' from seeing their goal literally above them.

Physical education is another important aspect of officer training, and both organised games and specific fitness tests are included in the course. All the main sports are introduced to the cadets, and competition is actively encouraged against their Sandhurst counterparts, and colleagues from the Royal Navy and other NATO forces. The level of each cadet's basic fitness is steadily raised in preparation for the leadership training phases of the course, which will involve setting up a camp in a suitable MTA (Military Training Area), sometimes in nearby Clumber Park, in Norfolk, in Yorkshire, or in Cumbria. Field exercises play an important role in the IOT course, and once the cadets are suitably briefed on the arts of knot-tying and map-reading, their skills are put to the test out 'in the field'. During the first camp, the flight will live for eight nights in permanent buildings actually on camp, with food provided. On the final camp however, the accommodation is rather more basic — under canvas — and rations form the food supply. The days spent on camp are physically very tiring, involving a great deal of cross-country travelling (on foot), and little time for sleep. The final camp is designed to represent a FOB (Forward Operating Base) for the Harrier force, and the cadets are charged with the defence of the area, putting into practice the skills learned at Cranwell.

The cadets run the administration of the camp, and organise patrols and 'attacks' on 'enemy' positions, spending some of their time working under NBC (Nuclear, Biological and Chemical) warfare conditions, complete with protective clothing and masks. They are armed with blank ammunition not only to add a touch of realism, but to impose the added responsibility of weapon security. Whenever possible the RAF also provides some aerial support in the form of helicopter transport, and sometimes delivers rations by Hercules, even providing the odd attacking aircraft. It sounds like a recipe for fun, and in many ways it is, but the excitement is tempered by the exhausting nature of the exercises, and the knowledge that the training has a very serious purpose: the cadets might have to work in these conditions 'for real' during their RAF careers.

Instructors record the cadets' performance during each part of the course, building a personal file on each student as he progresses. If extra training is required in specific areas, it is given, and each cadet is given a full debrief after every exercise he participates in. In many of the exercises his fellow cadets will be encouraged to voice their own thoughts on an individual's performance. The woodlands surrounding Cranwell are generally full of cadets clambering over obstacle courses, as each trainee is given the opportunity to lead an exercise, in much the same way as Biggin Hill conducts the hangar tests. Here, however, the instructor tells the individual where he made the right move or made a mistake. The cadets add their own comments too.

The mid-course review is an important milestone at which the Flight Commander discusses the progress of each cadet on a one-to-one basis, establishing each individual's strengths and weaknesses. The DIOT staff think it is important to inform each cadet of his progress, so that he knows which aspects of his performance he needs to improve during the second half of the course. Indeed, throughout the eighteen weeks at Cranwell, the cadets are free to discuss any problems with their Flight Commanders. Towards the end of the course the performance of each cadet in the leadership training will be assessed. There is a required standard to meet, and those that fall short of the target are reviewed in detail. At this stage the Directing Staff could simply suspend the cadet from officer training, but if a basic leadersip potential is detected, the cadet will be 're-coursed' and sent to 'R Squadron'.

The ten-week R Squadron course is designed to encourage the cadets to develop personal qualities and attitudes that haven't become evident during the main course. 'On R Squadron we tend to deal with the cadets who just haven't been able to show their true potential during the main course. The IOT course is just eighteen weeks . . . probably the shortest of its kind in the world, and some just don't develop in the time available. We could put them back into the main course but they tend to put on an act, and they'll probably fail at the same hurdles again. We're dealing with the less confident.' Part of the re-course training takes place on a PET exercise (Practical Experience Training) at Grantown-on-Spey in Scotland. During a series of outdoor activities in the mountains and valleys of the Highlands, the instructors encourage the cadets to develop their self-confidence.

It's also a perfect opportunity to establish the true nature of each individual: 'You see, I couldn't say what you are really like just talking to you here, but if I took you up in the mountains for a few days, I'd get to know your strengths and weaknesses, and what you're really made of. Some of the cadets are over confident too, especially the ex-ATC warrant officer types, and the UAS students . . . some can be such cocky buggers and they think that they're going to sail through Cranwell, and it comes as a big shock when they fail. With that sort we get 'em to zip-lip . . . maybe try and get them into an embarrassing situation. We try to get them into the team spirit, helping others . . . looking after number one is no good.'

The work undertaken by R Squadron certainly gives good results, with almost a 90 per cent success rate, the cadets being transferred back to the main course for the last six weeks, to complete their academic studies. The final assessment at the end of the course includes the results of written examinations, and reports on the oral communication exercises, defence studies, physical education and personal qualities, including a final judgement as to leadership potential. Cadets who fall into the 'doubtful' category are referred to a review board, which studies their cases thoroughly before deciding whether the cadet should be suspended, re-coursed or graduated. Of course, some will 'VW' (voluntarily withdraw), and the DIOT puts nobody under any pressure to stay if his mind is firmly set against continuing. At the same time, every effort is made to encourage such cadets to think long and hard before withdrawing: 'A cadet might just have had a couple of bad days, so there's no point in making a hasty decision to leave.' There are always a few cadets, however, who do decide that their taste of RAF life hasn't been to their liking. Certainly, Cranwell is no holiday. Some simply cannot cope with the physical effort required to complete the course, and the DIOT is not inclined to keep cadets who genuinely wish to leave: 'Well, if a guy's completely sure he wants to leave, he's no good to us anyway, so there wouldn't be any point making anyone stay against their will.'

As one of the Directing Staff comments: 'Cranwell is a place to learn about yourself. We teach them a great deal, but by the end of the course we do treat them like grown-ups and we expect them to act responsibly. On the social side, things often don't come easily . . . they do put on a facade, and it's useful to see them in a more relaxed situation, at a drinks evening maybe, to see how they conduct themselves. You can sometimes see character traits, and we give them pointers. Dress is another point. We have a no-tarts rule . . . we allow them to bring along girlfriends to a function, but what they never appreciate is that it's up to them to ensure that their girlfriends are going to dress and act properly. The responsibility is on them, not their girlfriends. Like everything else, they have to learn . . . we work hard and play hard.

'We don't actively look for pilot qualities . . . we look for officer potential, and the qualities needed to be a pilot tend to lead across from the officer side of things. We're just looking for the minimum officer qualities. We have to keep an eye open for the DS-watcher, but ideally, the cadets should feel that they don't have to put on an act. They should try to be themselves.' The DS-watcher is a familiar breed. There are some cadets who manage to display great performances in front of the Directing Staff, but in a situation when they feel that they are not being watched, they sit back and let others take the initiative. Of course the DIOT staff have seen this sort of character many times before . . .

In the sense that no cadet competes against another, the IOT course is not competitive. The only competition is to reach the required standard to graduate, and official policy dictates that competition is to be discouraged, in order to promote comradeship and team spirit.

At the end of the course comes the Graduation Parade — a big day for the cadets and their families, who are invited to the passing-out parade, on the grounds in front of the famous College Hall. The importance of this day in the life of every cadet is summed up by the words of the reviewing officer: 'You have now attained a standard at which no lesser person than the monarch herself is ready to charge you with specific responsibilities as officers in her service.' Weeks of rehearsal culminate in a final ceremonial parade in full uniform, complete with rifles. The pride of the cadets is matched only by that of their parents, as the RAF provides its own salute in the form of a formation flypast. The flypast has become something of a tradition, and has been known to be rather lively: 'Oh yes, the Phantoms . . . they really were a bit low!'

Thus the initial officer training is completed. 'We accept that in an eighteen-week course we can do no more than lay the foundations and identify the potential and qualities required in a junior officer. We rely on further training and supervision in the Specialist Training phase to refine further the process which Initial Officer Training has begun. Nevertheless we cannot afford to set any less than the highest possible standards, in the certain knowledge that the initial impressions of the Service given here at Cranwell will largely determine the outlook and attitudes of these young officers for the remainder of their careers.'

Before they go on their separate ways, to the huge variety of specialist trades within the RAF, what do these young officers really think about their training so far?

'It's a great feeling to have completed the course at Cranwell. You can lose sight of the end, but I'd had the ambition to fly for years. I joined for the job variation . . . the job satisfaction. There's no nine-to-five routine and it's never humdrum . . . it's just not that way of life.'

'Some of it is a bit of a hurdle that you just have to get over. Well, at the time it was, but thinking back on it I'm not so sure . . . I wouldn't like to have to do it again, I mean, there are always some things that are going to be nasty, and some things you enjoy. Things like having to get up and bull the block and all that sort of niff-naff, which you never enjoy at the time, but looking back on it, it's no big deal really. There's a lot of hard work in it, a lot of physical work, but if you work hard at it you get through and you think that it's all over, it's okay.'

'Looking back on it, the things we did, like running round a field carrying pine poles and so on, you wonder what relevance that's really got . . . but you've got to be commissioned to get into the flying training. It helps that Cranwell is also a flying station, so while you're messing around with the poles and oil drums in the field all day, you're seeing the Tucanos flying around. I can certainly remember marching around on the drill square, and a jet comes over and really interrupts things, and I thought it was great — you know, I'll be doing that in a few more months' time . . . wish I was doing it now! . . . but it inspires you, you think oh, great stuff, that's what I'm here for really, and you watch it flying around, so it's always in your mind. I think the first couple of weeks were the worst . . . you always get a few negative thoughts then . . . after that, you get into the routine and just do it.'

An observer is also prompted to ask whether RAF life had turned out as the cadets expected it to be: 'Yes, I think things were really how I expected. In fact I thought IOT was a little easier than I'd anticipated. I'd heard all these horror stories about so much PE and running around, but you know, it was easier than that, I think. The thing that really attracted me was the BBC television series. I'd always wanted to be a pilot, but on the television it looked really good.' So why choose to be an RAF pilot? 'Well, I'd been in the Air Training Corps for a start . . . that was quite a big help, going around wearing a blue uniform twice a week, going on camp and things like that, it boosts your motivation I think. It's the job to do really . . . I've always liked flying. I can't say what the main reason is that I chose this career, there must be a hundred different reasons really. I love flying, it's a great challenge. The RAF itself is a good way of life, I think . . . it's hard to put your finger on the real reasons . . . It's the best sort of flying you could ever hope to be involved in . . . Why be a taxi driver when you can drive a Formula One? Why fly airliners around like buses when you can have the challenging sort of flying here, and get paid for it as well? Okay, the money isn't as good as in the airlines, but the flying's nothing like the same, is it? They have the pleasant shirt-sleeve environment and they get to see a lot of nice countries, but the flying itself is completely different, and they just sit there watching the instruments . . . this is a different ball-game altogether.'

3

LEARNING THE BASICS

The opportunity actually to climb into an aeroplane is still tantalisingly just out of reach as the newly graduated officers are sent to RAF North Luffenham in Leicestershire, for a short course at the RAF Aviation Medicine Training Centre (AMTC). As at Biggin Hill, more attention is paid to the officer's physical dimensions, and another set of measurements gives the AMTC a final confirmation of the pilot's compatibility with the aircraft cockpit. The new officers are issued with their flying helmets — the famous 'bonedome' and oxygen masks, all specially adjusted to fit the wearer as snugly as possible, without being too uncomfortable (although it has been said that the wearer's head is expected to change shape in order to accommodate the helmet). The officers push and wriggle their heads into the equipment, and sit bemused as adjusting screws are tightened. Inside the rubber mask and tinted visor, the wearer slowly comes

29

to terms with this peculiar (and rather uncomfortable) situation.

Out on the airfield, the students are introduced to the ejection seat rig: a 30-foot tower on to which an ejection seat is attached. Each student in turn is strapped on to the seat, and is given final instructions to keep his head well back against the headrest, and to give the firing handle a good sharp pull directly upwards. As he does so, the seat rockets skywards with a loud thud, and the student finds himself sitting at the top of the tower just a second later. It's rather like a particularly exciting fairground ride, but the rig does give the students a taste of what a real ejection is really like. The initial seat acceleration is rated at 8g — less than a third of the real thing, but it's enough to indicate what it's all about. To the uninitiated, ejection might seem like a relatively straightforward means of escape from a dangerous situation, but whilst the basic idea is simple, it's not a course of action that could ever be taken lightheartedly. Shooting into a 500 mph gale is no fun, and at 25g or more, the departure is likely to be swift, if not painful. A force equal to 25 times the normal force of gravity is a lot of pressure by any standards, and it is not uncommon for back injuries to be sustained. Nevertheless, the RAF judges (quite reasonably) that broken bones are better than being dead. Modern rocket-assisted seats allow aircrew to eject from an aircraft whilst on the ground, and without any forward airspeed, but a 'rapid egress' is definitely a 'life-or-death' means of last resort.

The lectures at AMTC are given by enthusiastic specialists, who relate stories of great horror with equally great glee, illustrating the harsh world of fast-jet flying. Hypoxia is a word familiar to all pilots, and its meaning and consequences are brought home to the students. Hypoxia (lack of oxygen) is an insidious and potentially fatal condition. It creeps over the victim quite unnoticed: 'The main point to remember is that you probably won't even know it's happening to you, unless you're able to recognise the symptoms.' The effects are rather pleasant, in fact, somewhat like an evening's drinking, and the victim's reactions are also similar to the effects of too much alcohol. Some assume a moody, almost nasty frame of mind, while others tend to become jolly, although whatever the reaction, the symptoms appear much more quickly than those connected with drink. Unless the onset of hypoxia is noticed fairly quickly, the victim simply becomes too 'drunk' to notice, and calmly falls into unconsciousness, quickly followed by a peaceful death.

The lecture contains some horrific descriptions, and introduces the prospect of being 'treated' to a demonstraton of hypoxia in the nearby decompression chamber — a large cast-iron cylindrical tank with a row of portholes along each side. Not surprisingly, it is known as the 'yellow submarine'. Decompression is another important part of aviation medicine. All fast-jets are pressurised, and obviously, the loss of an aircraft canopy would instantly cause the internal air pressure to decrease to match the external level. For the purpose of this demonstration, the instructor informs the gathered students that the pressure inside the chamber will be decreased to the equivalent of that at 8000 feet, representing the pressure inside the jet's cockpit. Once set at this level, the chamber will then instantly decompress to an altitude of 25,000 feet, representing the effect of the loss of a canopy (or a similar catastrophe) at this height. In terms of air pressure, the group inside the decompression chamber will quickly move through an ascent of 17,000 feet. The interior of the chamber looks like the cabin of an aeroplane, with two rows of seats and accompanying headsets and oxygen masks. The attending doctor informs the students that when the decompression is initiated, they may feel sudden stabs of pain in their stomachs or ears, above their eyes, or behind their noses. Toothache is another symptom. The cause is simple: gases inside the body will rapidly expand as the air pressure decreases and, unless they can quickly escape, the results can be painful.

The door to the chamber is sealed, and slowly the air pressure hisses down to 8000 feet, at which point the 'ascent' is stopped. A slow countdown and a sudden burst of noise heralds the rapid decompression. The noise quickly subsides, as does the thick mist which has instantly filled the room. Suddenly everything is icy cold. It's all over, and the students blink above their oxygen masks as they adjust to the sudden aches that have taken hold of them. All the occupants of the 'yellow submarine' are now dependent on the oxygen flowing through their masks, as the air around them is now so thin as to be of little use to any human. The doctor invites each student in turn to remove his mask, to experience for himself what hypoxia feels like. After taking a few breaths they realise that sudden suffocation isn't going to be their fate, and that the ordeal isn't so bad. Each student is then asked to draw a small picture on a piece of paper, and to write the alphabet backwards. Such a seemingly simple task, and with a feeling of great confidence the student fills his paper with letters. Slowly, however, eyesight becomes rather blurred and the student notices that his heartbeat is racing . . . apart from that, everything's fine, but oddly enough it does seem to be taking a little time to remember which letter goes where in the sequence, but no problem . . . keep going . . . The instructor calls for the oxygen mask to be replaced, and the student sits back, his face flushed, possibly feeling a little dizzy. And as for the alphabet? What went wrong? The letters are not in order, and the picture is nothing but a scribble. And what was that number the instructor asked to be remembered? Although the obvious proof of incapacity is serious, the students find the whole experience most amusing, especially the chance to watch their colleagues make equal fools of themselves, writing such nonsense, as their fingernails and lips turn blue.

Another subject concerns 'g'. The force of gravity has a profound effect on the human body, and in a high-performance jet a pilot can instantly find himself under the force of over six times normal gravity. Six g is rather hard to imagine; one's arms, legs, and head suddenly increase their weight by a factor of six, and the whole experience has been described as 'a bit like being sat on by an elephant'. Putting a fast-jet into a tight turn produces a centrifugal force that directs itself vertically through the aircraft. The pilot is forced down into his seat and his blood supply drains away from his brain towards his feet. With a force greater than about 4g the pilot will begin to experience tunnel vision: 'You still see things clearly, but objects on the periphery merge into a sort of grey blur, and it gets to a stage where you seem to be looking through a tube.' If the force isn't decreased a complete blackout follows: 'You just can't see anything at all, a bit like a grey fog, but you can keep turning, as you're still fully conscious.' In order to combat this effect, a pair of anti-g trousers is worn. These contain inflatable bladders which squeeze the wearer's legs and stomach in an effort to stem the flow of blood away from his brain. The system does work, but only offers roughly 1g's-worth of support: 'Even so, it gives you something to push your muscles against, which does help a great deal.'

The demonstration of disorientation is also a great source of amusement. A light-tight box containing a student is designed to rotate slowly, putting the unsuspecting occupant into a gentle acceleration — so gentle that he doesn't even know whether he's moving or stationary. The revolutions are reduced, inducing a slight deceleration, and the student is asked which way he is moving. Sure enough, he insists that he is moving in a direction completely contrary to reality. When the box is spinning at uniform speed, he says that he is stationary. With some clever use of light displays, the instructor demonstrates how one's perception of perspective and position can be instantly fooled in such circumstances: 'The human body is excellent for functioning in a 1g environment, but it's pretty useless in any other circumstances.' The occupant of the revolving box is instructed to place his head between his knees, resulting in groans of instant nausea and much hilarity for the onlookers, but, as ever, the entertainment has a deadly serious message. The staff of the AMTC make great efforts to impress on the students how easily one can become disorientated; if you can't see where you are, there's little value in flying 'by the seat of your pants', and only the aircraft instruments can be relied on to give a faithfully accurate picture.

The lectures continue, covering every aspect of flying and medicine, and the subjects are many and varied: how a common cold can cause complete incapacitation, how vaccinations are needed in order to visit some countries; the hazards of smoking, drinking and obesity; the importance of exercise; and much more.

Visitors to North Luffenham inevitably leave with a much more informed view of what fast-jet flying is all about. To some it can be quite a sobering experience to learn that today's pilots are expected to work in a potentially lethal environment, even in peacetime.

At long last, the students are at the end of their initial training and ready for the commencement of their flying instructions. Many students will have little or no flying experience, and for a first taste of this they are sent just a few miles away from Cranwell to RAF Swinderby, a small and fairly peaceful airfield where the De Havilland Chipmunks of the EFTS (Elementary Flying Training School) are based. A small number of each intake will have had sufficient flying experience to bypass the EFTS altogether, and they are sent directly to a BFTS (Basic Flying Training School) to begin flying the Tucano. To be eligible for this 'short cut', one must already have at least 30 hours of flying experience. A significant proportion of students who meet this criterion come directly from the Royal Air Force's UASs (University Air Squadrons).

There are sixteen UASs located around the UK, responsible for the flying training of university students who have expressed an interest in joining the RAF. There are two ways in which young men (and women) can apply to be accepted into a UAS. Firstly, there is a university cadetship scheme, whereby the student commits himself to an RAF career, and is thus commissioned as an acting pilot officer (APO), after undergoing selection at Biggin Hill and a short preliminary training course. The student is paid a salary and, upon graduation from university, moves dirctly into the RAF. Other students join the UAS as cadet pilots (CPs), afer passing interviews, and although the UAS may seek to accept those with an interest in the RAF and aviation, CPs do not have to commit themselves to an RAF career. A CP can expect to spend up to two years with his UAS, on a strictly part-time basis, as the RAF recognises that the UAS activities have to take second place to the university academic studies. The amount of flying time on the UAS basic trainer — the Scottish Aviation Bulldog — generally reaches about 65 hours after two years, while APOs generally complete a third year with the UAS, finally leaving with at least 95 hours' experience on the Bulldog. Roughly 30 per cent of any squadron's membership will be cadet pilots, and from these, perhaps half a dozen will decide to join the RAF, while the majority of the remaining personnel will be APOs, already committed to their career.

The new arrivals at Swinderby often find themselves renewing an old friendship with the faithful 'Chippie'. Many aspiring pilots inevitably join the Air Training Corps (ATC) during their school days, and the RAF operates a large fleet of Chipmunks on behalf of the ATC. Almost every ATC cadet is given an opportunity to fly in a Chipmunk at a local airfield, and thus this venerable trainer is no stranger to many students. However, flying the Chipmunk at Swinderby isn't simply a source of enjoyment as it was in ATC days. The function of the EFTS is to give the students a basic instruction in the techniques of flying an aeroplane, effectively serving to 'weed out' those who are physically unable to come to terms with the task. Until 1987, students were sent to Swinderby on a six-week course, consisting of fifteen flying hours on the Chipmunk, simply to be assessed as potential pilots. The FSS (Flying Selection Squadron) operation worked well, but further studies indicated that this first introduction into the flying environment could be used even more constructively, and now the EFTS aims to teach, rather than just select.

Obviously the RAF is keen to establish at an early stage which students are likely to make successful pilots, as the flying training process is a long and expensive undertaking, and it is far better to withdraw the 'training risks' sooner rather than later. Current estimates suggest that the total cost of training a fast-jet pilot is approximately

£3 million, and, as one might expect, great care is taken to ensure that such large sums of money are spent very wisely. Thus, the role of the EFTS is quite an extensive one, aiming to give each student a thorough training on an inexpensive aircraft, during 64 hours of flying spread over sixteen weeks. Normally eight or nine students form the basis of each of the new courses, which commence on six-weekly cycles.

'We test the ability to absorb instruction . . . We don't attempt to grade the students now, but if they don't come up to standard they are still chopped, certainly . . . They still have to pass each stage.' The EFTS instructors are keen to explain the advantages of their sixteen-week course: 'What we effectively have is a low-cost flying training school . . . before the new system started, the students went away and moved straight on to the Jet Provost, which was an expensive way to do things. We indirectly grade students here, if you like, and it's fair to say that if you can get through EFTS you're likely to be successful on the Jet Provost. The new system certainly is cost-effective. We understand that the saving over the old methods is about seven hundred thousand pounds per year, which is quite significant.'

The first flight comes after a period of ground instruction, and is essentially a familiarisation flight lasting roughly 45 minutes. On the second flight, the Effects of Controls teaching begins, demonstrating the use of rudder, ailerons, elevators and throttle. The student, who sits in the front seat, watches as the instructor demonstrates the effects of the control surfaces and throttle, before repeating each exercise as directed. The introduction is a patient and gentle one. By the fourth flight the student is being introduced to other activities, such as 'Straight and Level' (keeping the aircraft on a steady course, using the controls and trim), and taxi-ing. The art of control on the ground is by no means simple in an aircraft such as the Chipmunk. With its tailwheel undercarriage, the pilot does not have a direct forward view and has to rely on a Spitfire-style 'weave' down the taxiway, checking port and starboard clearances in turn, in an attempt to negotiate the airfield successfully without hitting anything. The gentle use of brakes and power is a skill which has to be carefully learned, although the expanses of the relatively uncluttered and traffic-free airfield at Swinderby do make life easier for the students.

By Exercise Seven, the variety of aerial activities has increased further, to include climbing and descending turns and stalling: 'We gradually expand the exercises, handing more and more responsibilities to the student, so he gets more and more to do. The instructor is there to resolve the mistakes, but the basic job is to demonstrate and then let the student repeat the action . . . He sees the instructor do it first, then he has a go himself.' The basic skills are learned quickly, but often after a great deal of work: 'Things like accelerating and decelerating aren't as straightforward as they sound . . . It's like a child learning to walk for the first time, simple things like learning to use your feet on the rudder in association with the throttle, keeping straight and level.' Each flight includes revision of techniques learned in previous exercises, and thus the learning curve points remorselessly upwards. Take-off and landing practice, and flying around the airfield circuit, are exercises which are repeated time and time again, in preparation for the first main hurdle the student has to face — his first solo flight.

The first solo generally takes place in Exercise Thirteen (the EFTS instructors are apparently not superstitous), and the student is required to fly the Chipmunk safely around the airfield circuit, unaided by the normal voice from the back seat. It sounds like a simple task, and it is, but for the student pilot it is an important milestone: 'Nobody thinks they will ever go solo, but they inevitably get there . . . What we have to ask ourselves as instructors, is whether the student is capable of going solo, whether he can simply cope on his own.' The Chipmunk isn't the most difficult aeroplane to fly, but it is quite demanding: 'It needs to be worked at.' The 145 hp piston engine is started by cartridge and, after carefully progressing to the runway, the aircraft quickly gets airborne at about 60 knots, climbing away at 70. Nothing happens too quickly in the Chipmunk, however. At about 800 feet, the aircraft is turned into the downwind leg and round on to finals, with flap selected down, and speed dropping away to 50 knots as the Chipmunk drifts over the runway threshold. Some careful control is needed to keep the aircraft straight on the runway, and on take-off there is a distinct sideways swing to control (a characteristic common to piston-engined tailwheel aircraft). However, in most respects, the Chippie is the perfect vice-free basic trainer.

If any proof was needed that the Chipmunk is indeed an ideal primary trainer, one only has to note that the aircraft has been in service with the RAF since 1949, and looks set to continue flying for many more years to come. One of the EFTS Chipmunks has the distinction of being the oldest aircraft in current operational service: WB550 entered service in November 1949 and has been flying at Swinderby since 1974, and its days of useful flying are by no means numbered. The EFTS instructors are experienced members of the RAF, all able to boast many years of service operating a wide variety of aircraft types around the world. The QFIs (Qualified Flying Instructors) generally work with particular students throughout the duration of their courses, and don't see much value in 'pooling' their resources: 'We like to put one instructor with one student to assist in the learning process . . . It helps if the student has to relate to just the one instructor. It also helps to give a better judgement of how a student performs overall . . . If the instructor kept changing, it would be difficult to get a full picture of how good or bad a guy might be.'

If, however, a student suddenly finds that life is becoming difficult, the staff will change the QFI, in order to be sure that the student isn't suffering from a personality clash with the instructor: 'We will change to a different instructor, and we are able to give a few more hours to sort out any problems.' Giving a student extra attention is referred to as being 'on review'. The QFIs regard this process simply as an intensified period of instruction, and it doesn't necessarily mean that the student is going to fail. The students, however, inevitably view such action with great suspicion, and begin to fear that their stay with EFTS isn't going to result in success.

There is a certain amount of mental pressure built into the course, chiefly because the flying exercises are constructed to expand the abilities learned in the preceding sortie: 'You find yourself learning one skill, and the next time you fly, you're expected to do that without any problem, and to be able to cope with something new. When you start, you think, bloody hell, I'm never going to make it, but I'm sure everyone enjoys the course . . . we live on adrenalin here.'

For about 25 per cent of each intake, though, the EFTS will prove to be an insurmountable hurdle and their military flying career will be over: 'For some guys it's a big blow, a cherished dream since childhood gone out the door . . . We explain everything of course, but even so, you can't take on a guy who's going to go out and kill himself.'

Halfway through the course, the capabilities of each student pilot will have increased enormously. Having come to Swinderby with no flying experience, they are now learning to put the Chipmunk into spins, steep turns, barrel rolls and stalls. They will have started to move away from the immediate vicinity of Swinderby, navigating as well as flying. The basic skills of control are now taken for granted, and each flight involves more complex manoeuvres, together with additional responsibilities, such as fuel monitoring, radio communication, and emergencies, such as an 'EFATO' (engine failure after take-off). 'We will expect the guys to put the content of the sortie together in an intelligent manner, not just fly the aircraft. Things never happen the way you plan them in flying, and the pilot has to be able to look after himself. However, we don't expect anyone to be perfect . . . we learn where the imperfections are. Some come here never having flown before at all, and it can be harder for them to settle down, but all we ask is that they make reasonable progress. The failure rate isn't high at all . . . If there is one thing which causes a student to fail, it's the lack of ability to cope with more than one thing at a time. They might not be able to change speed and direction, and talk on the radio at the same time. Some just can't hack it. It's not a continual test, it's more a matter of developing abilities . . . We're here to help the guys, not chop them, and we do our very best to get the ability out of them.'

The course is divided into sections, each containing a number of specific skills which are taught to the student. The skills are practised and finally tested at specific points ('critical points'), or during the Flight Commander's Check Flight and the Final Handling Test, at the end of the course. The few failures that do occur, tend to happen at the first solo stage, or during the Flight Commander's Check. The length of each sortie is laid down in the course syllabus, generally averaging about one hour. Students normally fly three sorties per day, although much depends on weather conditions, and sometimes a whole day can be lost to bad weather. The QFIs work even harder than the students, and can total four sorties on some days. Even when conditions prevent flying, the learning process continues on the ground, in lectures or private study. 'There are exams to pass, and the ground instruction is as important as the flying. The meteorological package includes education on all aspects of weather, such as the atmosphere, clouds, winds and so on . . . We have to explain what the sky can do to you . . . It's very important when you could literally have your wings torn off. You have to avoid thunderclouds, hail, dangerous air currents and so on. Really it's a mini forecaster's course . . . a lot of very dangerous conditions exist . . . things like airframe icing can be lethal.'

The second half of the course continues to develop the basic skills, while introducing more complications. Navigational exercises become more elaborate, with triangular routes, and solo flights away from the airfield. Instrumental flying comes into the syllabus, with instruction on how to use the complete instrument layout and 'limited panel' flight. The basics of formation flying require the students to develop the skills of station-keeping, breaking and re-joining formation, and turning in both line-astern and echelon formation. Eventually the student will fly formation solo, keeping station with the instructor's aircraft, through a series of climbing, descending and turning manoeuvres. Navigational skills culminate in 'unplanned diversions', requiring instant decisions from the pilot.

'The Chipmunk is tricky to fly accurately, which is why it makes such a good trainer. It develops the necessary skills . . . it's quite a testing little aeroplane . . . it's been used to train for the Spitfire, and it does the job at EFTS very well. Look at WB550 which has been around since '49 . . . it was the second production aircraft, so it's really an ancient piece of kit, but as good as ever. We wouldn't take something like a Cessna, simply because it would make life too easy . . . you'd stooge around like a car driver, which is no good at all. The Chippie has no great merit, but no vices either. The Bulldog could chop through cloud and do something on top of it certainly, whereas we're limited . . . if the cloud is low, we can't fly. We do teach a great deal to the students, but it's only enough to get a foothold on the ladder . . . airmanship is important, just learning the rules of the air. Instrument flying involves explaining and demonstrating how all the dials work. They have to learn to navigate and map-read on cross-country flights, and you expect them to be able to fly to a destination and know the arrival time, fuel state and so on. They must plan a course and fly it, even with things like wind changes . . . some just sit there dumbstruck. We look at each skill and try to determine if they have 'em all.'

The final flight in the course is the FHT — the Final Handling Test. Rather as in a driving test, the examiner will require the student to perform a series of manoeuvres during a one-hour sortie: 'The FHT really encompasses everything in the course, and the student will have to fly the aircraft well and perform the basic aerobatics and navigation exercises we've taught him, as well as cope with emergencies and so on. For the aeros, he'll be expected to do loops, barrel rolls, slow rolls, rolls off the top of a loop and so on . . . he'll be expected to put them

41

all into a sequence in an intelligent manner. He'll have to look after the navigating himself and comply with the usual flying rules, not flying below certain heights, etc. We'll throw in things like radio failures, closing the throttle . . . all sorts of things. There's no set rule except that there will be surprises . . . it keeps you sharp and on your toes . . . various emergencies will be thrown at him, like oil pressure falling, engine fire, all the things which need a decision.'

Flying and academic exercises aside, the students also have to come to terms with their new responsibilities as officers. 'It's not as bad here as at Cranwell, where you're watched all the time, but we're still judged on our officer qualities . . . things like looking after the desk in here, and the Battle of Britain day, when we're the hosts. . . . You aren't under any great pressure, but you have the moral obligation not to let the side down . . . It's much more relaxed here, though.'

The successful students leave Swinderby to join one of the Basic Flying Training Schools, putting their newly acquired skills to work on the Tucano and, although the prospect of flying a jet aircraft might be rather daunting to the EFTS students, the instructors are confident that the training at Swinderby ensures that the students will be able to cope with the transition: 'The Jet Provost and Tucano training format is essentially the same, simply an expanded version, but with the same basics. The QFIs here at EFTS are all very experienced, and we've all instructed on other aircraft, so we know how the training system works. We all have experience in different areas.'

4

FLYING TRAINING SCHOOL

Having learned the basics of flying at Swinderby (or with a University Air Squadron), the students are posted to a Basic Flying Training School. Three such units exist, these being No. 1 Flying Training School at RAF Linton-on-Ouse, 3 FTS at Cranwell, and 7 FTS at Church Fenton. The experience gained on the Chipmunk or Bulldog is now put into practice on a completely different machine. The pilot training course effectively comes full circle, and the students find themselves beginning with the basics once more, repeating exercises on a faster and more responsive aircraft.

Since the late 1950s, basic flying training has been conducted on one aircraft type, the Jet Provost. But in 1990, a new aircraft type entered RAF service, and it will eventually replace the faithful 'JP' in the training role. The turboprop-powered Shorts Tucano bears little similarity to its predecessor, and its new 'high-tech' design outperforms the Jet Provost in almost every respect. The content of the BFTS training courses is expected to remain essentially the same, however, aiming to train students to operate a relatively high-performance aircraft with confidence.

The long lines of red-and-white painted Jet Provosts at the FTS bases have long been familiar sights to passersby. The airfield circuits are continually active with 'circuit-bashing' aircraft, and the prospect of getting airborne excites every new student as he arrives at his new posting. Unfortunately, the first five weeks at a BFTS are spent firmly on the ground in a period of concentrated education concerning the technical aspects of the Jet Provost (and more recently the Tucano), as well as more general airmanship. The facts and figures which need to be memorised are many and varied: engine start-up and shut-down, engine 'flame-out', re-lights, hydraulic malfunctions, birdstrikes, radio failure, electrical systems, cockpit instrument layout, airframe icing . . . Before a student can take any aircraft into the air, he has to understand in minute detail the way in which the aircraft functions.

A QFI explains how the training system operates: 'The Ground School runs on a sort of package basis, in that it is the same for every course, and is designed to fit into an initial period of five weeks. The students work at their own pace, which includes a great deal of evening study, as there's a lot to learn. In fact there's about two hundred hours' worth of work to take in.'

After completion of this period, the course concentrates on flying instruction, the initial period being aimed at getting the student through the first major 'hurdle' on the course — his first solo flight in the Jet Provost. The basics are re-applied, exploring Effects of Controls, take-off and landing. Gone is the piston engine, and gone too (at least as far as the EFTS students are concerned) is the Chipmunk's tail-wheel. For the first time, the student is sitting on an ejection seat, equipped to punch him out of the cockpit upon initiation.

'So, having arrived at the FTS, they'll first go to the

Ground School, but during this period they will be given a familiarisation flight, and we'll take them into the air for half an hour or so, just so they can see what it's going to be like.' The instructors have a matter-of-fact attitude, but for the students, their first flight in a Jet Provost is an exciting experience, getting airborne in a distinctly military aircraft for the first time . . .

'If we have to eject, always go for the seat pan handle, as it's very difficult to reach the face-blind handle on the top. When a second could mean the difference between surviving or being killed, it does matter. On the command "Eject, eject, eject", get your head well back into the seat headrest, and give that handle a good hard pull.' Looking out at the world through a visor, over an oxygen mask, from inside a heavy and cumbersome helmet, the conditions are very different from those in the Chipmunk and Bulldog. The take-off isn't impressive, however, as the Jet Provost doesn't boast a particularly powerful engine, and the acceleration is gentle: 'Okay, we're rolling now . . . it is accelerating, I assure you . . . A little pressure on the stick and we're airborne. Undercarriage coming up.'

Safely into the air, the JP settles into a typical transit speed and altitude of 250 knots (almost 300 mph) and 250 feet. Looking out at the surroundings, one can see the world flashing by . . . fields, villages, rivers, hills . . . It's exciting, but certainly not frightening. Aerobatics offer a greater thrill and, after climbing to altitude, the instructor turns the little JP through a wide circle, checking the surrounding airspace for conflicting air traffic. The sky is a deep blue, and completely clear. It's a good place to stay a while and admire the scenery, but suddenly the world turns upside-down: 'Into a slow roll now. Here comes the horizon . . . round she comes . . . Okay? Don't forget to let me know if you're feeling unhappy.'

The nose pulls upwards and the landscape slips away under the aircraft, as the JP settles into a vertical climb, pointing directly upwards into the deep blue. The airspeed indicator confirms that the forward speed is decreasing rapidly, and while the instructor kicks the rudder foot pedals, the nose gently swings left and right: 'Now, which way is she wanting to go . . . ? Okay, we're turning to starboard . . . and over goes the nose.' For a brief moment, everything is stationary. The forward motion of the JP is perfectly matched by the pull of gravity, and the student and instructor hang motionless in mid-air, until the rudder inputs push the aircraft over into a stall turn, twisting round into a vertical dive, pointing down towards the distant greenery below.

'Just a little pressure on the stick, and round we go.' The nose edges even further downwards (but which way is down?) and the JP is pushed into an inverted oblique descent, the ejection seat straps and small dirt particles suddenly straining to push through the canopy, instead of the cockpit floor. The sensation of negative-g is peculiar, if not unpleasant. A gentle 'negative nudge' when driving over a hump-backed bridge is okay, but this is rather more severe and prolonged. Your instincts tell you to hold on to the cockpit wall, just in case you're pulled out of your seat, upwards (downwards!) through the perspex. Of course the straps keep you firmly in place. But tell that to your senses . . .

Back into an erect descent, the fields begin to look pretty close, and at the bottom of a long descent, the JP is pulled level, the g-force, now positive, pushing you hard into the seat backrest. With a bonedome on your head, it's an effort to keep upright. Never get caught with your head down when pulling g . . . you'll never get your head up again until the manoeuvre stops! The accelerometer reads '3' . . . only 3g. For a new student, that might seem impressive, but it's nothing. 'The clock says we should be heading home now . . . you have control . . . that's the heading we want, so try and keep us straight and level.' Over the airfield, a tight turn into the airfield circuit, down with the landing gear and flaps, and back on to the concrete. The delights of such introductions serve to fill the students with enthusiasm for the long training period, which lies ahead.

'On the actual course, we start off with the basic teaching exercises like Effects of Controls, moving on to straight and level, just learning how to maintain straight and level flight.' The teaching is built up with a full briefing before each flight. 'They'll go off into a cubicle and they'll cover all the aspects of the flight, the type of exercise, and basic airmanship points . . . rather like if you're in a car, the basic road-sense. It's not just the mechanics of flying, it's being aware of all the other factors, such as lookout, who is in control of the aircraft, orientation and checks like oxygen, fuel, and that sort of thing.'

The students are tasked not only with the control of the aircraft, but also the management of the on-board systems too, chiefly the fuel supply. As the exercises progress, more and more responsibility is put directly on to the student: 'On the initial sorties they will be told to check fuel about every five or ten minutes, but the instructor will obviously have a careful eye on it all the time. In the early days, the student is concentrating so hard on all the other aspects of the flight, that he forgets about fuel management, so we try to get them into a routine of regularly checking. They should also check the oxygen supply, that the engine is operating properly, their location, and so on. This is all briefed for the sortie, and also during mass briefs, where we get all the students together and go through all the basic points of a forthcoming exercise.'

The BFTS course sets a series of specific aims for each training flight. For example, a typical sortie could include demonstrations of the way in which the aircraft controls are used, how the ailerons affect the roll rate of the aircraft, how the rudder controls the yaw, and how the elevators (the tailplane) affect the pitch, pointing the aircraft upwards or downwards. The initial training is very simple, teaching the student how the Jet Provost and Tucano 'feel' to the hands and feet of the pilot. Even the act of getting the aircraft off the ground and into the air requires a good deal of practice: 'You will have to show the guy how to taxi out and line up on the runway, with all the appropriate lookout, and the use of the RT. He'll have to call for take-off clearance, get on to the runway, get the power on slowly, up to ninety per cent, and then make sure he remains stationary at ninety, as that's the brake check. Then up to full power, brakes off, rolling down the runway, keeping it straight initially with the brakes, and then with just the rudder. By 85 knots you increase the back pressure on the control column, and the nosewheel should be off at about that speed, just settled on the mainwheels, and then at 95 knots the aircraft will fly off. Then there's the gear and flaps to be raised, engine checks to do on the climb, and more RT to leave the airfield circuit . . . and so it goes on.

'Further on in the course you get them to change speed, because on the earlier exercises they will have been flying at just a set speed. Now they have to fly straight and level at varying speeds, accelerating and decelerating. Climbing and descending, and circuit turns, normally done at height away from the airfield . . . and then we come back and maybe do a couple in the actual circuit, at the end of the sortie. Then we have a look at stalling the aircraft, how to recognise a stall and how to recover from it with minimum height loss. If the student gets into a low speed situation when he's close to the ground, he's got to be able to recognise the stall symptoms and be able to make recovery action. The main thing to look for is a high nose angle or a low decreasing airspeed. The controls will become very light and sloppy, and there will be airframe buffet too. We teach them to recover clean, with no gear or flaps, and also how to do it 'dirty' — with everything down, putting on the power, overshooting, and raising the gear and flaps.

'Then there is some continuous circuit-bashing, doing roller landings, talking to air traffic, flying co-ordinated turns on to finals, lining up on the runway at the right place . . . just building up their confidence. When they have reached a safe standard, we will fly a Dual-to-Solo, flying with the student, then after half an hour we land, get out, and the chap goes off on his own. You have to satisfy yourself that he's done about three circuits safely . . . they don't have to be incredibly accurate, but the main thing is safety all the time. It's all very subjective, and it's up to the QFI to judge when the student is ready to go solo. He'll do just a quick circuit, taking off, into the circuit, turn downwind, approach and land, and that's his first solo. After that we do more consolidation, building in glide circuits. Should he have an engine failure, he should be able to glide back to the airfield. For a forced landing we would set up a simulated engine failure away from the airfield, then glide in, achieving a position called High Key, gliding to the Low Key position at the end of the downwind leg at fifteen hundred feet, then turn in for final approach.'

The next major stage in the training syllabus is known as Sector Reconnaissance. This is the first time that the student pilot is briefed to fly solo away from the home airfield, to gain a degree of familiarity with the local area surrounding it. The pilot is given a simple route to fly over the local countryside, using basic navigation techniques, and after flying the route accompanied (at a height of 3000 feet), he then re-flies the same course on his own. 'After that phase, the student moves on to more advanced stuff, like flying step turns, flying at sixty degrees angle of bank, spinning the aircraft, learning how to position himself for entering a spin, how to recognise spin symptoms, and how to recover. They will not spin solo, at least not intentionally, but when they're doing aerobatics later in the course and things go wrong, it's possible to enter a spin. So they need to know how to get out of it.

'Then comes the solo General Handling flight. Obviously monitoring a solo is difficult. You know what the guy is like, and you've given him a thorough briefing before he goes off, and explained all the rules and regulations he has to obey. You just expect him to go and do as briefed. He's trying to pass the course so it's up to him to go and practise. There's no pressure, the solo is just his opportunity to practice without an instructor sitting next to him. After this comes an introduction to instrument flying, followed by aerobatics . . . initially the basic five, which are loop, barrel roll, roll off the top, stall turn, slow roll . . . and also a wing-over which counts as an aerobatic manoeuvre. We encourage them to practise these as a sequence, linking them together.'

If the student doesn't successfully complete a specific part of the training course, he will be allocated additional hours of flying training. A small amount of extra flying instruction can be given, when required, to compensate for occasions when the student encounters difficulty. Sometimes, however, it may be that the novice pilot is simply having a 'bad day', something which can be expected occasionally, and a condition with which the instructors are very familiar. 'On the Spin Aerobatics test, the student will organise an hour's sortie, plan it, and then fly with an instructor, to see if he can safely depart the circuit, do turns, stalls, aerobatics, a spin and recovery, recover from unusual positions, and fly some circuits back over the airfield, doing a radar recovery. If they fail and do extra hours, they can then have another go at the test. If they fail that one, there will be progress reports written on the chap, and he may go to Review Action, which means that we keep a special eye on him. He'll maybe get a more experienced instructor, and maybe extra hours to help him. We find that people encounter problems at various stages on the course, but if there's a specific exercise where he isn't coping, we have what we call flex-hours, which are used as required.

'The Gate is simply one of a series of tests, essentially to weed the guys out . . . with an off-squadron examiner sitting next to the student, with the accompanying additional pressure. The guy has to present his sortie to the examiner. However, assuming that they do pass that gate, they do more solo, practice aerobatics, navigation at medium level, then a long period of instrument flying, building up their capabilities so that they can fly around with a lower cloud base. Then there are UPs, or unusual positions, in which the instructor induces an excessive angle of bank or a high rate of descent while the student isn't looking, which simulates what would happen if the student had looked into the cockpit at some switch, and stopped scanning the instruments properly . . . He looks up and sees that the aircraft isn't in straight and level flight, so he has to take the correct recovery actions. That all leads up to a basic instrument flying grading, allowing him to fly in slightly poorer weather conditions.

'When the students have flown around fifty hours in the Jet Provost or Tucano, the course has reached the halfway stage. Their course now begins to incorporate more advanced aspects of training, such as the use of various radio navigational aids, and low-level flying at 250 feet. The capability to fly at low level with confidence and safety takes time and some thorough demonstrations from the instructors. The skill has to be developed to judge height visually without relying on the altimeter, which cannot be relied on due to pressure variations. The instrument flying is built upon further, so that the student is capable of flying to a diversion airfield if necessary, bringing in instrument approaches, and Precision Approach Radar, working towards the next rating in the course.

'Then it's more maximum rate turns, flying the aircraft on the buffet, to the maximum point of lift. The buffet comes on when you're just approaching a high speed stall, the maximum amount of lift that the aircraft can achieve. If you go into a turn at 220 knots, pull into light buffet at about five g, the speed will decrease and stabilise at about one hundred and fifty knots and two g or so . . . and you maintain that on the buffet. If you over-pull, you go into a high speed stall, but to recover from that you just have to release the back pressure on the stick. Further down the course comes a full low-level navigation sortie, more instrument work, and then the Advanced Flying Test, which allows the students to descend through a greater depth of cloud, and fly approaches under Surveillance Radar control. We then combine high level navigation with the low level navigation, and do a mixed profile Navex [navigation exercise]. The Basic Handling Test at the end of the course involves the student showing the examiner just about every aspect he has been taught, and then he is ready to go on to the next stage of training.'

At this stage, the student will be role-selected and,

depending upon abilities and preferences, will be streamed into one of three groups. Group One, which includes students destined for fast-jets, means flying another 60 hours on Jet Provosts or Tucanos. Group Two students fly another 15 hours before moving to RAF Finningley for multi-engine training in the Jetstream, and Group Three students are transferred to helicopters — though these latter are often selected at an earlier stage of the course. The Group One fighter/bomber hopefuls continue their training at the BFTS: 'Having completed the basic course, the students will go on to night flying, night navigation and practice diversions. The night flying skills are similar to those required for instrument flying, but there are stages where you have external references to keep the aircraft in the right place. The students have to develop this ability, as they tend to be staring at the instruments when they could be looking out, but at other times it can be very disorientating if you're looking out . . . maybe there are stars, and pinpoints of light on the ground, so you can't tell where you are.'

There follows a solid period of basic handling and instrument flying, prior to flying an Instrument Rating Test, which qualifies the students to use the airfield Instrument Landing System (ILS). The speed of low-level navigation flights is increased to 300 knots, instead of 240 knots, which the students have previously been accustomed to. A lengthy period of formation flying is then undertaken, some twelve sorties, using two or three aircraft combinations: 'We fly basic positioning, breaking away, re-joining, and basic turns. As their competence improves, they do higher angles of bank, and more severe manoeuvres. Tail chasing, formation circuits, approaches and landings, formation in cloud. After that phase we return to low-level navigation, normally on detachment to places like Brawdy, Leeming, Kinloss or West Freugh, somewhere close to hilly terrain, so that they can practise valley flying, contour flying, leading to a Final Navigation Test. Before that they will also have done some land-aways, going to another base, doing a turn-around and flying a different route back. On the test they will have

a target included on the route both inbound and out-
bound, to which they will have to locate the IP — Initial
Point — and fly down it, over the target. After that there
is more GH revision, leading up to the Final Handling
Test . . . the very end of the course.'

Deciding which type of operational aircraft the student
would be best suited to is a difficult task for the instructors. There are no specific rules to dictate which students
would be better suited to fast-jets, multi-engined types
or helicopters. The decision is subjective, relying on the
instructor's experience: 'We have to ask ourselves what
the guy is really like, whether he is switched on with the
right sort of temperament. For fast-jets, we have to decide
if he is aggressive enough, whether he gets on with the
job, how he reacts under pressure. For example, if his
instrument flying is good but he can't fly too well at low
level, he might well still make sound decisions, just
maybe needing a little more time to cope with the situation. In that case he would probably go to Group Two.
If he can fly at low level but can't handle the aircraft too
well, he may be better suited to helicopters, where he
will be re-taught to handle that type of machine. We
always take note of personal preference. We don't push
people to join Group One, but we try to get people to go
that way, because that is the type of pilot the RAF needs
most of all. However, if the guy has a definite preference
for something else, he will probably go on that route.'

In between the flying exercises, the students will spend
a great deal of time studying in preparation for their next
exercise on their course. General Service Training (GST),
first introduced at IOT, is still continued, albeit on a
reduced scale. Ceremonial drill is still practised, as is
fieldcraft — learning how to survive in potentially hostile
territory. Every course features a Landex — a week-long,
outward-bound style course including long-distance
walks, making a shelter, and finding food. The capability
to survive alone is important for wartime operations, but
even during normal peacetime training there are many
unpopulated areas of the UK where a pilot could, in an

emergency, find himself ejecting into adverse surroundings.

The BFTS course is long and full. The students have a
great deal to learn, and many simply do not make it to
the end. Problems can be concerned with almost any
aspect of flying; simple co-ordination of control column
and throttle is a common pitfall. Airmanship, remember-
ing checks, navigation, formation keeping, night flying,
low-level flying, circuit flying . . . all are potential areas
for failure. Every aspect has to be mastered with competence, and even for the most able of students it's very
hard work. A typical post-exercise debriefing illustrates
the problems: ' Right, the taxi-ing . . . don't stamp on the
brakes, keep going in a nice straight line. You must learn
to anticipate before the marshaller. Would you agree with
that? Okay. Now, the take-off . . . the line-up was done
nicely, but at take-off speed it was obvious that things
were not going well. Try to keep the ailerons neutral
unless there's a wind on one side. You can play around
to find a neutral position . . . look out of the front a bit
more. Notice the way it slopes down; in fact you'll find
that the ailerons will work on the ground, against the
oleos. You don't want such a nose-high attitude. When
we got off the ground we started to waver, and yet you
don't do that on your rollers.'

The debrief continues, with the instructor raising many
points for the student to consider and act on: 'On the
manoeuvring I reckoned it had to be better than last time,
as we didn't get into heavy buffet. Now, on this bit of
navigation: How did we get Harrogate after Lincoln?
Now, remember you don't have to slam the throttle, and
if you try rolling while stalling, the aircraft will depart.
Don't hold it in the buffet for too long . . . yes, I know
we didn't get the nose drop, but why bother? Why wait
for the nose to drop? Look, what's the number-one symptom of a stall? Yes, heavy buffet, so why wait for the
nose to drop? Now, this navigation . . . You will have to
sit down with a map, put some radials on it from Pole
Hill . . . so what does Pocklington look like? No, without
looking at your maps . . . No, we were never anywhere

near Pickering . . . you said Pocklington . . . oh, you meant to say Pickering . . . What can you do with these chaps?! . . . What was the rate of descent there? It was nearly off the clock, and we don't want to be like that at two thousand feet or we'll impact. Now, back here, point your aircraft at the deadside of the runway, not Leeds . . . and keep looking out of the cockpit, because the Cessna pilot isn't going to see us until it's too late. And then on finals you have got to cut power, otherwise we won't go down. Don't start searching for the runway, just cut the power, check, hold, and wait . . . The taxi in was okay. Well, overall the sortie wasn't too bad; you can't expect everything to come together at once . . . Is that a fair account of what went on? . . . Okay.'

There is a justifiable sense of achievement in completing the BFTS course. The syllabus is extremely demanding, and the failure rate is fairly high. Those who do make it can look forward to exercising their skills on an aircraft much faster and much more agile than both the Jet Provost and Tucano . . .

5

FAST AND LOW

Originally formed at Abu Sueir in the Egyptian Canal Zone, No. 4 Flying Training School was responsible for the training of pilots destined for service in the Middle East, equipped initially with Avro 504s, later receiving Avro Tutors, Hawker Harts, Auduxes and Armstrong Whitworth Atlases, the latter being used form Army co-operation flying. Two days before the outbreak of World War Two, the unit moved to Habbaniya in Iraq, a fairly large airfield with a wide range of facilities, just fifty miles from Baghdad.

By the beginning of 1941, training schemes in Southern Rhodesia and South Africa were producing significant numbers of newly qualified pilots, and 4 SFTS (redesignated as a Service Flying Training School to avoid confusion with an Elementary Flying Training School) was effectively redundant. Plans were made to disband the unit, but on 1 May the FTS was transformed into an

57

improvised operational unit, in response to political developments. During the previous month, a German-supported rebel by the name of Rashid Alid had seized power in Baghdad, together with four generals of the revolutionary Iraqi Army.

The Regent Abdulla Illah fled to Habbaniya, and was subsequently moved to safety, while Britain, in an attempt to protect its oil interests in Persia and Iraq, immediately sent troops to Basra, near the Persian Gulf. Rashid Ali, infuriated by this move, decided to flex his military muscle, and deployed 9000 troops plus artillery to the south of Habbaniya. Thus, 4 SFTS became the 'Habbaniya Air Striking Force', with a mixed fleet of Auduxes, Oxfords, Gordons, Gladiators and a Blenheim. The number of rebels in the area continued to increase, and following a warning to withdraw (which was not heeded), action commenced against the rebels on the morning of 2 May. Five days of continual attacks against the rebel positions followed, during which 4 SFTS flew 584 sorties, dropping 45 tons of bombs and expending 100,000 rounds of ammunition. By the morning of 6 May, the rebel positions had been abandoned.

Fighting continued, largely against attacking Italian and German aircraft which turned their attentions on Habbaniya, but at this stage four Hurricanes from No. 94 Squadron were brought in to assist with the conflict. Following the collapse of the last rebel stronghold at Falluja, Rashid Ali and his associates fled to Persia, Baghdad being captured by British troops. Thus, 4 SFTS had not only successfully defended Habbaniya, but had turned the tables on the rebels, leading to their ultimate defeat.

Fifty years later, 4 FTS is still very much in business, at RAF Valley, on the Island of Anglesey in Wales. All prospective RAF fast-jet pilots are posted to 4 FTS after successfully completing basic flying training on the Jet Provost or Tucano. The first Tucano graduates arrived at Valley in October 1990, and from this date onwards RAF Valley expects to receive students from both aircraft types until the Jet Provost is completely replaced by the Tucano in the basic trainer role, in the early to mid 1990s.

Towards the end of their basic flying training, the students are 'streamed' into one of three categories, depending upon their own wishes and their individual capabilities. Group Three covers helicopter types such as the Puma, Chinook and Sea King. Group Two includes the 'heavies' (Tristar, Nimrod, VC10 and Hercules, etc.), while Group One is fast-jets (Tornado, Phantom, Harrier, Buccaneer and Jaguar). As the commanding officer of No. 4 FTS's Flying Wing comments, 'We are a kind of nursery for all of the Royal Air Force's fast-jet pilots, and every student streamed into Group One will come to us here at Valley.'

No. 4 FTS's Flying Training Wing has a strength of roughly fifty flying instructors and around sixty students at any one time. The unit is divided into a number of squadrons. Standards Squadron, with a strength of around ten instructors, has two functions. One flight prepares categorisation for the unit's QFIs, while the other flight is responsible for staffing the three flight simulators at Valley. The students fly 21 full sorties in the simulator, ten of which must be flown before going solo in the 'real' aircraft. No. 1 and No. 2 Squadron are both flying units, situated on the northern side of the airfield, close to the station administration and engineering complexes. No. 3 Squadron, another flying unit, is located south of the main runway, purely as a symptom of Valley's widely scattered aircraft flight lines, which trace their locations back to the days of the Hawker Hunter and the Folland Gnat. Both types were utilised by 4 FTS simultaneously, prior to the introduction of the BAe Hawk in 1976. The fifth squadron, Ground School, has a staff of five.

Apart from regular RAF students, 4 FTS also teaches a smaller number of foreign and Commonwealth students, as well as Royal Navy pilots, destined for the Sea Harrier Naval Air Squadrons. Also included in the annual intake of students are ENJJT (Euro Nato Joint Jet pilot Training) scheme pilots, who arrive at Valley after completing basic flying training with the USAF in Texas, flying the Cessna T-37. A shortened 50-hour Hawk course is flown by each of these students, in order to 'Europeanise' them after having become accustomed to USAF procedures. Out of each year's throughput of BFTS (Basic Flying Training School) students (at Church Fenton, Linton-on-Ouse and Cranwell), five will go to Texas for training. As the Wing Commander explains, 'Texas is almost continually eight eighths blue sky, so when the students come back here they've hardly seen any cloud, and we try to get them used to our weather conditions again. The Americans also tend to be more procedure-oriented than we are, so we have to reintroduce them to our way of doing things.'

The Wing Commander continues: 'We also re-role people, maybe the chap who has been a Jet Provost QFI now going on to fast-jets, and we'll give him a twenty-five hour course here. We also deal with refresher flying, for instance for some of our own students who may have had to wait a fairly long time between completing their course here and starting at one of the Tactical Weapons Units. So we'll give them four or five hours of flying, before they start the TWU course.' This variety of flying courses results in a total of around 15,000 flying hours per year for the school. Consequently the 4 FTS instructors can expect to fly around thirty hours per month, with some maybe even reaching 40 hours.

A group of eight to ten students begins a course every two or four weeks, and at any one time there are seven courses in progress. One course will be in Ground School, while the other six are divided between the three flying squadrons. Each course spends the first five weeks in Ground School, with 165 hours of intensive study to prepare them for the equally intensive flying syllabus. The Ground School phase includes a variety of subjects such as aircraft operations, survival training, general service training, defence studies, physical education, oral and written communication, moral leadership, etc. Within this phase the students will complete the initial ten hours of 'flying' in the Hawk simulator.

Included in the simulator instruction is a considerable amount of standard procedure training. The general principles of ATC (Air Traffic Control) procedures, for example, will be essentially the same as those found at any

RAF station, but local operations do require specific changes to normal rules and regulations. Because of the proximity of RAF Mona (RAF Valley's Relief Landing Ground), the Valley ATC circuit pattern is often very busy, and Valley has a unique transit system of one-way routes to get aircraft to and from the airfields safely. With the introduction of more and more Tucano graduates, Tacan (TACtical Air Navigation equipment) approaches are also becoming a more regular part of the initial simulator training. Quite naturally, the eager students would happily dispense with five weeks of ground studies but, as 'The Boss' says, 'they simply have to do it.'

Following this phase, the students are allocated to one of the three flying squadrons to commence a 17 to 18 week course, flying 76 sorties, equal to a total of 75 flying hours on the Hawk. This results in each student normally flying one sortie per working day. The first 30 hours of flying is a conversion phase including pre-solo instruction, instrument flying (achieving their first Hawk instrument rating), general handling and so on. The applied phase follows, after each student has flown a 'check ride', to ensure that they have grasped everything that has been taught and that they can fly the Hawk sufficiently competently to move on.

The Wing Commander explains: 'The applied phase is really where all the hard work is done. Starting with general handling just to keep the student up to speed, we include five hours of night flying, and what I suppose is the real meat of the course, the formation flying, both close and tactical formations, and navigation exercises, where we range around a wide area of the country at four hundred and twenty knots and two hundred and fifty feet. Also included is some free navigation, IP-to-target routes and so on. It's very demanding but it's very exciting too. We try to go through all of this on a dual-solo-dual-solo basis, so that the students get plenty of opportunity to practise their captaincy of the aircraft. We're reasonably flexible with these exercises because of the weather. So if it's not a low-level navigation kind of day, we might go upstairs, get above the clouds and do

some instrument flying. We can change things arund a
limited amount in this way, but we have to make graduation dates, of course.'

Indeed, one of the reasons why Valley is the home of
4 FTS (and has been for 30 years) is because of the station's good weather record. Should the conditions be
particularly poor, however, aircraft are regularly
deployed north to Lossiemouth, Kinloss or Leuchars, to
take advantage of weather conditions in other parts of
the country. Returning to the content of the course, the
Wing Commander continues: 'The students become very
competent at flying formation while they're here. We'll
take them up to about three g and one hundred and
twenty degrees of bank at three hundred knots, and they
can hold position very well. We also teach them tactical
formations, in pairs down at five hundred feet, flying
level turns, and although we don't teach them to led
formations while they're here, we do have them sitting
in the back seat of the Hawk on two sorties watching the
instructor lead a formation.' With the introduction of the
Tucano, students will already have greater experience of
leading formations, so it is quite likely that 4 FTS will
make alterations to the syllabus eventually, in order to
accommodate the different (and better) proficiency of the
Tucano graduates.

At the end of the course, the students will fly a Final
Handling Test (FHT), a composite sortie including general
handling, instrument flying, low level navigation and formation flying. 'After the FHT they will receive their wings
here at a formal ceremony, with their mums, dads, girlfriends and so on, and during the afternoon we try and
get one or two operational aircraft types to fly through
as part of their training sorties, as the families tend to like
that. So we make the ceremony a full day for everyone to
enjoy. Following graduation they will go to one of the
TWUs, either at Brawdy or Chivenor, to do their weapons
training, before joining an Operational Conversion Unit.
One or two per course will be creamed off, selected to go
to the Central Flying School as a first-tour Qualified
Flying Instructor. The phrase "creamed off" is pretty

accurate, as they will be the ones who have come top of the course, guys with good flying ability and good personal qualities.'

The aircraft used by 4 FTS receives almost universal praise from both instructors and students. It is highly manoeuvrable, very economical to operate, affords a good view for both student and instructor from either seat, and is very serviceable. It has a 25-knot crosswind capability, which can be useful at Valley, as, despite having two operational runways, neither is aligned to the prevailing wind. Good use is made of the Hawk's 'long legs' too, using a huge MTA (Military Training Area) for medium-level and high-level work over Wales, and for an hour-long sortie, bases as far apart as St Mawgan in Cornwall or Lossiemouth in Scotland can be used as diversion airfields. After completing the sortie in the MTA, a last-minute diversion (because of bad weather or a blocked runway) allows the Hawk to reach these distant airfields safely: 'We can overshoot from Valley with five hundred kilos of fuel on board, and land at Lossiemouth with two hundred kilos still left.'

For low flying, virtually the entire country can be used, apart from the scattering of restricted areas highlighted on every pilot's maps. Navigation sorties regularly take the Hawks down into Devon or up into Scotland. Practice approaches are made to many RAF airfields, together with civil fields such as Ronaldsway on the Isle of Man, Liverpool and occasionally Blackpool. The seemingly endless range of the Hawk is used and valued by 4 FTS. The Hawk is stressed to positive 8g, and for day-to-day flying, 6g is the maximum figure permitted (and regularly used): 'It's a tough aeroplane and a real joy to fly at low level. If I had to make any criticism of the Hawk, the only thing I could say is that perhaps it's a little too good. Maybe it's not demanding enough in some respects. Certainly it has no handling vices at all, it's very difficult to spin it, it's very controllable in the stall, and it has good all-round vision.'

Listening to the 4 FTS instructors, the attributes of the Hawk are certainly greatly appreciated, but the course is certainly no joy ride. 'The Hawk is a very easy aeroplane to fly, but some students just can't cope. They've come here after flying the Jet Provost, and compared to that machine, the Hawk is like the Space Shuttle. There's not much time to think in this aircraft, so you can get into trouble more quickly. The first familiarisation flight is with the student in the back seat. It's just a jolly really, done during the Ground School. At roughly the halfway stage in the Ground School they are about ready to get into the aeroplane, but it's really a Staff sortie, and they start the course proper on Exercise Two. As with the EFTS and BFTS courses, the first flights deal with the effects of controls, leading to stalling and basic aerobatics. As the students now have a basic flying ability, these first flights in the Convex (Conversion Exercise) Phase progress quickly, and by Exercise Four the student will be performing the start, take-off and climb, and flying to a diversion airfield.

'The syllabus hasn't really changed since we had the Gnat. The students are not going to do anything significant until we get on to Effects of Controls, when we'll demonstrate something, and then they have a go at doing it. We can't afford to let them try and take off, as they've got used to flying the Jet Provost, which just about needs both feet against the control column to move it; whereas on the Hawk, it's so very light. The first time they get a crack at the whip therefore is with the Effects of Controls. If the student's showing a reasonable degree of skill, and he's keeping up with what's going on, we can just talk about things while he flies them, but obviously when you start doing circuits we have to demonstrate a couple. The first one will be very basic and we'll just talk it through, but on the next one you actually go to power settings, speeds, attitudes and then he'll have a go at one . . . then we just build from there.

'For much of this early work we have what I call "monkey-see-monkey-do" sorties. Basic aerobatics involve a loop, barrel roll, slow roll, aileron roll, that sort of thing. The student will have done plenty of emergencies in the Hawk simulator, so on Exercise Six we have a minor emergency and recovery. We give him something that he has to think about — fly the aeroplane, carry out the appropriate drill, and consider what he's going to do to get back home. So we're starting to develop his airmanship more to see if he can cope with something unusual. He'll end up doing a Progress Check, which is a test to see how his general handling is, and very soon afterwards, or possibly before, depending on the weather, he'll do some instrument flying, ending up doing an Instrument Rating; whereas if the weather's good, he'll concentrate on his general handling, leading to the Progress Check. He'll do both within a week or fortnight of each other, so he's then qualified to fly the Hawk in cloud, and then he can get on to the really interesting stuff.'

If the student fails to pass the Instrument Rating Test or the Progress Check, the review action begins, and the examining staff try to determine whether the problems are purely a symptom of test nerves, or something more fundamental, such as simple inability: 'Some get test nerves, others just find that on the day they aren't as good as they could be; but by this time the QFI will have a good idea of his ability, so we can normally determine what the problems are. If we decide he's okay to continue, we give him a couple of spare sorties, maybe up to four if he needs them, and then he'll go for another test — a pass-or-fail flight. So we bring him back up to speed, restore his confidence, and give him another crack at it; and if he fails, that's it really. The writing is on the wall with the second test, because if he fails then, there's little point in continuing as he'll probablly just struggle on and fail somewhere further down the line.'

The Progress Check occurs at Exercise 28 and the IRT is normally scheduled for Exercise 30, concluding the basic Convex Phase of the Syllabus, with 20 hours 40 minutes flown dual and a further 8 hours 40 minutes flown solo. The remainder of the course forms the Advanced Phase, starting with a lead-in to night flying. The times at which the night flying is brought into the course vary depending upon circumstances. Although the syllabus is divided into rigidly numbered sorties, the exercises do not have to be flown in numerical order, and, like the earlier IRT and Progress Check, the various elements can be moved around to suit the course: 'Sometimes it could even be that the guy's finished the whole course, done his Final Handling Test, and then goes back to do the night flying. Each sortie is marked on its relative merits, so if he flies one bad sortie in isolation we can look back and see if there have been any problems earlier in the course, but the QFI should be able to determine if he's just having a bad day. Exercise 38 is a birdstrike lesson, where we teach the student what to do if his aircraft should be struck by a bird of some sort, an accidental event which can cause a huge amount of damage. We teach the student to get up away from the ground and then try and determine what's happened.' More and more solo sorties are introduced into the course, intended to reinforce the student's confidence: 'You can't really debrief these solos, and you don't grade them. The only way you can do that is to launch another aeroplane, and follow him round. We do that every now and then, but it's not a rigid part of the syllabus. If you have someone you're a little unhappy with, then on the solo nav you send a staff instructor along in another aeroplane. It also helps to see if they're looking out . . . if they notice this aeroplane in their mirror. That way, they can't just taxi round to the back of the hangar and make appropriate radio calls: we can catch 'em out!'

Exercise 51 is the Final Navigation Test, which is a simple pass-or-fail event. There is no specific final formation test, but it is incorporated into the FHT, the Final Handling Test. Throughout this period the students are working towards the end-of-course examination, when their newly acquired skills will be tested in detail. The FHT is the culmination of months of intensive training. 'We do let the students fly some general handling in the middle of the formation and navigation exercises, but there's always five or six more at the end to work up to the FHT. These days it's a front-line orientated sortie, so he could go off as part of a two-ship, do a tactical formation, break away and go solo, do some low-level navigation, then some medium-level turning, aerobatics, and some circuits . . . so we see a full spectrum. We could give him anything, really. He will probably have a fair idea of what the route is going to be, or we could just give him an IP-to-target run, but it does depend on what the examiner feels like doing, within the syllabus. If you gave the same test to every student, they would know what to expect, so you wouldn't really be testing them . . . The only purpose of that would be to check their ability to reproduce a specific sortie, and you can't do that. The weather changes things and you have to be flexible. It could be a beautiful day and you'd do tactical formations followed by low-level navigation, but on a really poor day you would check his ability to do Instrument Flying . . . go off and do a diversion somewhere, come back for a PAR or ILS approach. On the front line where they are eventually heading, they've got to be able to do anything, any time. If we can't generate that ability to think flexibly even now, then we're wasting our time.'

As the instructors explain, with experience it is relatively easy to spot a number of potential faults arising, when students inevitably begin to fall behind in the training schedule: 'It could be a basic handling ability problem, being unable physically to fly an aircraft in close formation. Maybe he can't recognise when the situation is changing, and respond in the correct manner. If you then go and look at his file, you'll probably find that he suffered the same problem during basic flying, and they've just got him up to a basic standard. We expect more and more ability from them when they get here, so a weak student who is on a level learning curve at BFTS is just going to fall off here. Sometimes somebody pretty average at BFTS can really take off here, just because he's been fired with some sort of enthusiasm which he didn't have earlier in his career flying a JP. Alternatively you get a Mr Average who is the same at BFTS, here, TWU and at the front line, when suddenly he "clicks" and gets it together. You also get the ones who are good at the BFTS and good here, get creamed off and become good flying instructors too!

'Fuel awareness is another important aspect. If the student doesn't constantly monitor his fuel situation, he may not notice if he begins to use fuel faster than planned. Obviously he must be sure that he can get home with sufficient fuel, so he should make an effort to do something about his problem, such as truncating one of the navigation legs, or climbing out of the low-level phase earlier than planned . . . or maybe even turn back and divert to another airfield. At least that means he is aware of the fuel state, and has made a positive move to land somewhere. He will be expected to think in those terms from a very early stage in the course, certainly before his Progress Check.' Other points which the instructors consider include poor navigation and flying too low. Every student is expected to be able to see how the terrain flows, and be able to react to the relative height of the ground over which he is flying. Sitting at 250 feet, letting the hills come up to meet him, and then fall away, is simply unacceptable. He must maintain 250 feet over the hill and down the other side. 'The biggest problem is that they just sit there with the map in their hand all the time, navigating, instead of putting the map down. The key to low-level navigation is to be able to put the map down and not look at it. It's not as ridiculous as it sounds, because if you've got a leg, say, eight minutes long in a straight line, providing you're flying the speed correctly and the stopwatch is running, you will get from A to B in the prescribed time, and you will arrive there, notwithstanding any crosswinds. You might have a twenty-knot crosswind and a seven-miles-a-minute speed, so you may want to come into wind by about three degrees. Certainly you would still get to within a mile of your destination.

'We try to convince the students to do a work cycle of about four minutes, as you wouldn't expect them to put the map down for eight minutes. You'd pick up the map and remind yourself, about a minute before an event, then maybe a fuel check and postiion check on your straight line. You then pick the map up again just before you reach the point, and there it is, on time . . . maybe ten seconds slow, so you up the speed, or you re-judge what time you're going to get to the next point. Once you can convince them that putting the map down is not a recipe for disaster, they can look out for other aircraft and become more aware of what's going on around them. If by about Exercise Twelve in the nav bit the student's still looking at the map, and then up, straight through the windscreen, and never looks over his shoulder, then he is not confident at low level.' The instinct is to over-read the map, paying too much attention to the charts, and insufficient attention to the world outside, where visual cues to the route flash by. The instructors try to cure the tendency: 'It would be like a guy starting on a motorway and saying that he wants to leave at exit twenty, and at every exit checking if he's at number twenty or not . . . instead of thinking that it will take, say, one hour and fifteen minutes to get there, so I'll start worrying about it in an hour. Of course, the motorway journey's taking place at a much slower speed over a much longer distance, but it's all relative. I can be as far out after seven minutes as you can in your car after an hour, which is why our work cycle is much faster. When you come to a turn for instance, you manoeuvre and then have a confidence check to make sure you're still in the right place, and if you're not, then look at the map.

'In the free navigation exercises, you're not on a set route any more, so you would pick mountains, lakes or comparable features, and you'd then have to instantly look back to your map and determine at what point you went wrong, to work out where you are, or might be; and you have to decide all this in roughly the same amount of time as I've taken to tell you, because at seven miles a minute you're going seriously wrong, seriously quickly . . . seriously! So the first point is not to get lost! What you have to say to yourself is: Did I get the heading wrong at the last turning point? Answer yes or no. If no, then where the hell am I? You're bound to know, because if you're ten degrees off your heading you must have diverted from track, and you're going to be seven minutes out or whatever, and ten degrees right of track, so you have a quick look at what is round about that point, maybe a lake or a little town.' Keeping one's eyes looking out of the cockpit is the essential skill. It's vital to keep a continual visual check on external reference features, which can be interpreted against the map's predictions: 'You look out and find the town, and okay, you know where you are . . . you now make a correction to go left maybe ten degrees to bring you back parallel, and another ten degrees to get you back to your next turning point, and there you go . . . you just accept that you're going to get back to your turning point. Or you could say, I should be over that place on that heading, so you just rack the aeroplane round and get it into that place and track. There are a number of ways you can sort yourself out, but the assessment always has to be from the last place at which you knew where you were. You look at the map . . . make sure you haven't cocked it up during the planning stage, like putting the reciprocal heading down by mistake, or the magnetic variation the wrong way, with seven East instead of seven West so you're fourteen degrees out and don't know it . . . you've got to think about things like that when you're on the ground so you don't have to worry about them in the air.

'The number of times you sit in the back and ask them how they're doing, and they say they're okay and on track. But how can they be, when they're ten degrees off heading? You can see them holding the map and looking down, instead of looking at the instruments, keeping them right and looking outside for other aeroplanes and the next turning point.'

The course becomes even more difficult as it progresses, and most of the failures occur at the Progress Check, or shortly afterwards. Some do not proceed beyond the first solo, but even so, the overall 'chop' rate is quite low, at about fifteen per cent. A student explains: 'If I get chopped here, at least I will probably have somewhere to go, as very few get chopped altogether. They normally go to Group Two or Three. They deserve not to be chopped by this stage, and in any case it's not the end of the world . . . some guys go to multi-engines and then cross over and come back here . . . it's not irreversible.

You need a much greater capacity here than you do for multi-engines, but even so, a posting to something like the Nimrod would be very enjoyable.' The emphasis is placed on flexibility, and the 'composite sortie' becomes the order of the day. No longer will a sortie explore just one specific exercise. The student must cope with more and more variety, culminating in his final flight — the Final Handling Test. Not only will the student be required to operate the aircraft efficiently, he will also have to plan and manage the sortie. And by now, the initial excitement of life in a fast-jet environment has inevitably begun to wear off.

'You do start to think about being chopped. I'd certainly accept another flying job, either Group Two or Three, or navigator. I'd hate to be back at the beginning though, treated like a schoolkid again. I like being in control. By the time you get to Valley, you either enjoy flying or you've got out, and you've learned the realities of your capabilities. As the course progresses you begin to wonder if you've got what it takes, you know . . . better to be doing a job you know you can do, maybe. The ground-flying syndrome sets in . . . it's not that you're frightened of flying, it's just that you'd rather be on the ground than be flying badly. No, it's not a fear of flying, it's a fear of failing. When things go well you think it's great, but when you start falling behind it's a very different matter. You have a much better idea of what it's all about by now, and you've an idea of what being a Harrier or Tornado pilot might be like, and you sometimes think maybe it's not such a good idea. Some guys do decide to pack it in.

'It's a satisfying job and we just want to make it where perhaps most people couldn't. Down in the valleys, the gaps get so narrow, and you're pulling six g round some of the corners . . . it's really exciting, and even if I don't make it, at least I've been there and I've done it.'

6

LEARN TO KILL

Successful completion of the Hawk course at Valley entitles the student to receive the coveted 'Wings' badge. He is now effectively a fully qualified fast-jet pilot. However, whilst the ability to fly an aircraft of such complexity as the Hawk might be considered as something of an achievement, the Royal Air Force demands much more from its pilots. Having developed the capability to fly the Hawk confidently, the students are now taught how to operate it as a weapon of war. From 4 FTS at Valley, the students will be posted to one of two Tactical Weapons Units (TWUs) at Brawdy in Wales (1 TWU) and Chivenor in Devon (2 TWU). Both TWUs share the task of training the students to operate the Hawk as a weapons system, rather than just a high-speed jet trainer.

From his office, looking out over a runway towards the nearby coastline, a TWU instructor explains the role of the two units: 'We teach the students the basic skills of combat, such as air-to-air and air-to-ground gunnery, low-level navigation, air combat manoeuvring and so on.' The sixteen-week course is even more demanding than the previous course at Valley, and the intense training offered by the TWU will enable the successful student to both fly . . . and fight.

'For a couple of years, both at Brawdy and Chivenor, we ran what was known as a streamed syllabus, whereby we found out how many slots would be available for ground attack or air defence, and then gave the appropriate number of students the corresponding course. However we have now returned to the way we used to do things, giving everybody the same course, and only at the very end do we direct them to specific front-line aircraft. We pushed very hard to go back to the common course because we believed that it produces a better result. For example, you finish up with air defenders who have actually experienced the other side of things, and they have actually flown Simulated Attack Profiles on ground targets, and so on. We're now able to be more flexible, as hitherto we could have streamed people to either mud-moving, or air defence, only to find out later that the chosen route wasn't the one they were best suited to. Now we can wait until the end of the course, the logical time to decide their future, and we can put the round pegs in the round holes. The combined syllabus doesn't cost us much more than the previous one, in terms of flying hours.'

This change in the TWU syllabus is a good example of training flexibility, and of how all aspects of training are constantly monitored and adjusted to give the most effective results. Although the aims of the streamed course were admirable, the results were disappointing. The students did receive additional flying time which was devoted to one of the two roles (fighter or ground attack), but they failed to gain an appreciation of the skills employed by their fellow pilots. For example, a fighter pilot learned little about the ground-attack pilot, and in a wartime situation the knowledge of his opponent's limitations could be vital. By experiencing some ground-attack

Above: The DeHavilland Chipmunk over RAF Swinderby in Lincolnshire, home of the Elementary Flying School. In the RAF's Air Experience Flight network, would-be fast-jet pilots first take to the air and find out whether or not they've got what it takes to handle an aeroplane.

Below: Tail chasing, during a typical Jet Provost training sortie. The lead aircraft is a T3A, with its wingtip fuel tanks, the rear aircraft a T5A, the later, pressurised version of the Jet Provost.

Above: An instructor's view of a Hawk tail chase. The black lines running through the canopy are part of the Miniature Detonating Cord system which instantly shatters the canopy prior to firing the ejection seat, when the escape handle is pulled. The British Aerospace Hawk first flew in 1974. It is highly manoeuvrable, reliable and relatively simple to fly, allowing a student to concentrate on flying the aircraft for a purpose rather than concentrating on controls.

Above: A 2TWU Hawk, dolphin-like, crossing the Bristol Channel at low level. The rippled fuselage skin illustrates the punishing regime in which the Hawk operates. It is capable of making 8g turns and, at the opposite end of the scale, an incredible − 4g, but no student is ever likely to put himself into that kind of flying attitude.

Below: The Harrier GR5 squadrons are high on many students' lists of first-choice postings. Harriers are strictly 'mud-movers' (offensive support or ground attack aircraft), but the GR5 can carry Sidewinders as a self-defence measure.

Above: A Phantom FGR2 heading back to the flight line, canopies open for a welcome breath of fresh air after a punishing aerial combat sortie.

Below: The Tornado GR1 has proved a formidable offensive support aircraft, with pinpoint bombing accuracy, long range and good reliability. It will eventually replace the Buccaneer in the maritime strike squadrons.

Above: Ready to roll. White helmets are rare, though some pilots prefer their heat-reflective properties, and in combat training sorties a white bonedome can be a useful eye-catcher on a drab grey machine. Needless to say, camouflage grey/green would prevail in a war.

Above: While aircrews' accommodation and briefing facilities may be protected from NBC (Nuclear, Biological and Chemical) contamination, a Hardened Aircraft Shelter (HAS) is not, so aircrew are equipped with their own NBC respirators to get them safely from the 'hardened' site to their cockpits.

Below: Groundcrew wearing full NBC gear, removing a Phantom's Sidewinder safety covers, prior to engine start.

flying, the fighter pilot can learn more about the way in which the bomber pilot, or tank-buster pilot, thinks, and use the knowledge to his advantage. Naturally the reverse applies too, and the ground-attack pilots learn how fighters operate, and so on. After a great deal of careful consideration, the TWU's returned to a combined course, and all TWU students now learn the same skills, equipping them all with the same degree of understanding and ability, producing a better 'all-round' result.

The TWU instructor (a former Lightning pilot) continues his description of the course: 'We operate two squadrons at Chivenor, and at any one time each will have two courses running within it. The course lasts sixteen weeks, and we get a new course starting every four weeks, so by using advanced mathematics you can see that we get through about twelve courses each year, with ninety-six pilots passing through.'

The first stage of the course is a Convex Phase, intended to ensure that each student can confidently fly the Hawk, rather than simply relying on 'paper' assurances from Valley. It is also important that all the pilots understand the TWUs SOPs (Standard Operating Procedures), concerning basic rules of safety, etc. 'Convex consists of a dual sortie involving general handling; a solo general handling flight, just to allow the student to become familiar with the local area; and one or maybe two instrument rides. In fact we often fly just one instrument ride which is in effect an Instrument Rating ratification, as they arrive here with a current Instrument Rating.'

The Convex Phase continues with formation flying: 'This begins with four sorties, starting with a dual flight, that is, pilot and instructor together, at medium level, which is then followed by a solo medium-level sortie. We then take them into low-level formation, with another dual, followed by a solo. The first two sorties involve a small amount of close formation, usually a formation take-off, followed by about fifteen minutes of close-up work, with a close formation recovery and landing. We then move to tactical formations, that's a battle formation, which they will have looked at while they were at Valley, but not very thoroughly; and we aim to give them a really good grounding in battle formation flying, as they're going to be using it throughout the course and, indeed, through the rest of their fast-jet flying career.'

Once the students have been thoroughly trained in the operations of the Hawk within a tactical environment, the instructors introduce the first part of the weapons phase. The Hawk shows its talons for the first time, as a bomb, gun, or missile carrier: 'We start with what we call Simple Cine. As you know, we have a gunsight fitted in the TWU Hawks, and we have also installed a camera which can film whatever is seen through the gunsight. With this we will fly a dual sortie and a solo sortie, following another aircraft, so that the student can get used to the idea of aiming his gunsight at another aircraft. There are only two trips of that sort, before we move to Cine Weave, which is slightly more complicated, in that the aircraft which is being chased will perform some rather more dramatic manoeuvres than on the first two sorties, while the student attempts to follow him and keep his gunsight trained on him. They will do one dual flight and then a couple of solos, and the resulting gun-sight films will be assessed. At the end of the flights they will receive a mark, indicating their ability to track another aircraft at the correct range. This is their first introduction to weapons, and although they're not firing anything other than photons, they are taking film.'

Although the Cine Weave sorties are assessed, it would be wrong to imply that all the other sorties are not care-fully monitored: 'Every flight will be written up. If the sorties are dual, the reports will be written by the instruc-tor who was in the aircraft. There are a few sorties that are not written up, however, for pretty obvious reasons. Solo general handling for instance. How could you pre-pare a report on that? On some of the later solos they will be monitored by an instructor who will follow in another aeroplane, and in reality very few sorties they fly here are not assessed in some way or other.'

Having mastered the techniques of high-speed navi-

gation at low level during the Valley course, the TWU
students are expected to develop their skills still further.
Looking through a detailed table of the TWU syllabus,
the instructor explains: 'At about the same time that we
introduce Cine, we bring in the navigation phase, our
aim being to have what we refer to as weather options.
If we're running a low-level phase, we also like to have
a medium-level phase at the same time, so that if the
weather is too poor at low level, at least we can do something with them, and of course the reverse applies, when
we encounter bad weather at medium levels. At the
moment, the low-level navigation phase consists of seven
sorties. One is just a check-out to ensure that they have
all the fundamentals right, and that they can safely fly
the Hawk at two hundred and fifty feet and four hundred
and twenty knots, these figures being the general minimum height and maximum speed on low-level flying
training over the UK. We normally fly sorties at speeds
which are multiples of sixty knots, because that's the
easiest sort of figure to use for working out timings. In
the Jet Provost or Tucano they will have flown at one
hundred and eighty knots or two hundred and forty
knots, which is either three or four miles a minute. They
might have gone up to three hundred knots too. At Valley
they will have started doing their Navexes at three hundred and sixty knots, which is six miles a minute, and
they will have finished at four hundred and twenty knots.
Here at the TWU we jump straight in at that speed. If
you went to a Tornado or Phantom squadron you would
find them flying at that sort of speed during a transit
flight. Obviously you could go much faster, but that
would use more fuel, and we would also cause even more
of a nuisance to people on the ground. You would be
using a higher power setting which would create more
noise, and we do try very hard indeed not to annoy the
general public. In the Hawk a speed of four hundred and
twenty knots is a useful cruising speed, and if we flew
any faster we would be rather hard-pressed. We could
aim for four hundred and fifty knots, but we would be
using full power almost all of the time, whereas we can

maintain four hundred and twenty up hill and down dale. Typically in our Hawks we need ninety-three or ninety-four per cen power to maintain the speed.'

The navigation exercises continue, with what the TWU instructors call 'Chase Navs'. For the first time in their careers, the students will fly in company with another aircraft which will not be in formation with them, but will be following their progress. From the vantage point of this chase aircraft, an instructor will watch the student, checking the height and speeds that are being flown: 'This puts a little bit of added pressure on the student, knowing that he's being watched all the time. We will carefully check the height he's flying, particularly if he's too low, as we would want to deal with that very quickly. We also see exactly where he goes on his navigation, while he flies a route that lasts about fifty minutes, including a couple of targets to overfly en route. One of the sorties will normally be a land-away, where he will recover the aircraft to another airfield, often near the east coast, at places like Coningsby or Cottesmore. Then we can fly the next sortie on the return to base. Next comes what is really a major progress step, Nav Four, which involves a pair of aircraft, usually with an instructor and student in each aircraft. On this flight the student will fly as a battle formation pair, not only flying the planned route, finding a couple of targets, but also doing the whole sortie in a defensive battle formation. We find that this is a particularly difficult sortie for the students, as they are already working very hard navigating and flying at low level, and now they have the additional worry of manoeuvring a formation successfully, to compound their problems. A good defensive battle formation is important, because it is the only way that the pilot can keep a good lookout to make sure that he's not going to be bounced — that is, attacked by another aircraft. By flying about two thousand yards apart, line abreast, they can check each other's six-o'clock area for any marauding aircraft which might be trying to shoot them down. On these particular Navexes we don't have anyone trying to bounce the formation, but it allows them to get used to this kind of operation, ready for later sorties when we will launch a bounce aircraft, to see just how good their lookout is. On Nav Four, one student will lead the formation until halfway, at which point the lead will be handed to the other student, which allows each student to spend half of the flight leading, and the other half formating.'

The next three sorties require the student to lead the flight, without the aid of a pre-planned route. He will be given a target, plus a fairly large mount of advice as to how the route should be planned, but exactly how he reaches the target is effectively his own decision. Once the route is planned, he will be expected to brief the pilot of the second aircraft, and lead the flight. On Nav Five a staff navigator (a TWU instructor) will fly in the rear seat of the student's Hawk. This will be the first time that the student has ever flown a dual sortie with a 'passenger', someone other than a flying instructor, introducing the practice of flying with a navigator, rather than another pilot, in the back seat. For the first time, the student will be operating his aircraft as a true two-man fighting machine. The pressure continues to build as more responsibility is transferred to the student: 'The workload gradually increases. On the days when you have good weather, your workload isn't enormous, as all you have to do is to keep looking well ahead to see where you are going, but in more marginal conditions it can involve a great deal of decision making on the part of the student, as he will obviously have to navigate around the weather. Clouds can have solid centres when you're flying low level.'

After completing the navigational exercises, the course returns to more weaponry training, with the introduction of the strafe phase: 'In this phase the student fires the Hawk's thirty-millimetre cannon at targets on the ground, normally on the weapons range at Pembrey in Wales, not far from Swansea. It consists of four sorties, starting with a dual in company with a QWI, a Qualified Weapons Instructor. Assuming that the student is judged as being safe, he is sent off to fly a Cine sortie, without any live rounds in the gun, simply taking film as if he were actually firing the gun. If that sortie shows that he is safe enough to be let loose with live ammunition, he will fly a further two sorties with real bullets in the cannon. Each sortie will be with fifty rounds, to fire at Pembrey's acoustic target. Upon completion we will record their score, and the film will be debriefed by a weapons instructor. After having seen the film, or if the range safety officer decides he wasn't happy with the way the sortie was flown, the flight could be DNCO'd as we say; that means Duty Not Carried Out. If that happens we make them re-fly the sortie, so even though they're flying solo, they are still being constantly monitored.'

Even at this advanced stage in the student's career, the pressure not to fail is still very high, and some students will find that they cannot keep pace with the TWU course: 'We don't have a dramatically high chop rate here, and on average it probably works out at about ten per cent. People do get suspended for a number of reasons, first and foremost being our concerns over safety aspects. It's not just that they obviously mustn't be at risk of writing off themselves, anybody else, or the aircraft, but we have to consider that we could squeeze through a student on this course only to have him kill himself and a navigator later on, in a Tornado or Phantom, doing God knows how much damage on the ground as well. So all the time the main point is safety. However, there are some things in the course that some people just can't cope with. They might have performed quite well until now, and then they come to a brick wall, as far as their progress is concerned. I like to think that we're a fairly caring unit, in that we wouldn't simply suspend a student unless we saw no further point in carrying on. We would aim to re-fly a sortie if we felt the potential for success was there. For example, we can look at the navigation phase: suppose that someone performs adequately until he gets to, say, Nav Five — and then got himself hopelessly lost, or flew dangerously, or maybe didn't show any due consideration to his fuel state, that sort of thing — we would probably re-dual him, and fly him on another sortie, with an instructor. We might send him off on another solo,

but not if there were any safety concerns in his performance. If we then considered him safe to be sent off on his
own again, he would try and re-fly the original sortie that
he failed.'

The flexibility and positive nature of the TWU syllabus
is reflected by the series of gradual steps that can be taken
to bring a student back 'up to par' without suspending
him from training: 'If, after that stage, he still hadn't got
what it takes, we would put him on review . . . which is
a way in which we can highlight the fact that we've got
a problem. And this enables us to give the student some
more flying hours. We would give him a little remedial
package, maybe two dual Navexes or something like that,
and during these sorties we would monitor his progress.
Throughout we would aim to be pretty flexible, but if by
then the student still appeared unlikely to crack it, we
would probably chop him at that point. If he did show
even a glimmer of potential, we might send him off on
another solo, and maybe give him the benefit of the
doubt. It's not a rigid, laid-down procedure whereby we
say that the student has got maybe two more sorties to
make good and then he's out. Every case is treated on its
merits.'

Returning to the core of the course itself, the training
continues: 'Also within the basic phase is some night
flying. While they are at Chivenor they will normally fly
three night trips. They will have done this before at
Valley, so we start with a simple dual to check their
safety, and then on to a solo, followed by another with
plenty of instrument work, runway approaches, a practice diversion to another airfield, maybe a couple of
emergencies and so on. We usually fly these spread over
two nights. Then, finally in the basic phase, we move on
to ACM, or Air Combat Manoeuvring, the basic skills of
the fighter pilot. Before this the chaps will have spent
some time on the Air Combat Simulator at Coningsby,
flying a number of sorties in their twin-dome simulator.
This will give them a basic feel for ACM, and it will tend
to make their progress rather quicker when they get into

the air. We then start them off with two dual sorties to teach them the basic combat manoeuvres.'

The students now begin training in the skills of aerial warfare, learning how to become fledgling fighter pilots: 'It's important to remember that combat is completely new to them. They are now fighting against another air-craft, trying desperately not to get themselves shot down, and whilst they will have flown tail-chases, this is a whole new concept to them. At this stage we will be simulating gun-armed aeroplanes, positioning the aircraft between three and five hundred yards behind the target aircraft, within the effective range of the Hawk's cannon. Again the use of the camera will simulate the gun, and show the student how he is going to shoot down the other guy. If the first two dual sorties are judged to be safe, they will then fly three solo one-versus-one sorties, fighting with an instructor. Tucked in somewhere in the middle of the course will be what we call a Tac-IF check, where we take the guy up on a dual sortie and throw some emergencies at him, check out his instrument flying capa-bilities, and make sure he hasn't been developing any bad habits, and so on.'

Following the ACM phase, the students return to oper-ations in the air-to-ground role, flying ten-degree dive bombing sorties over the Pembrey range. As ever, the first sortie is flown dual, then with a cine camera, and then two further sorties carrying live practice bombs: 'We then progress to what is called Bombing and Strafe, where we not only give them four bombs to play with, but fifty rounds of ammunition in the cannon as well, and they will be given a half-hour slot on the range in which to drop the four bombs and fire the fifty rounds. They will be given two such combined sorties. The next flight will be a level bombing sortie flown dual, followed by three "hot" sorties where they are actually dropping bombs. The practice bombs are released at four hundred knots, at a hundred and fifty feet over the range. How-ever we never fly below two hundred and fifty feet when we're off the range. I might add when we're flying at two hundred and fifty feet, on the Navexes, the height will be judged visually, as naturally a pressure altimeter is no good whatsoever in that sort of environment, when the terrain varies so much.'

Following this phase, another general handling and instrument flying sortie is included, with an instructor in the Hawk's rear seat. There then follows a formation sortie, usually flown with four Hawks, serving to refresh the student's formation-flying skills, learned earlier in the course. Two low-level evasion sorties follow (one dual, one solo), in which two aircraft will be flown around a low-level route in battle formation, with a third Hawk acting as 'bounce' aircraft, assuming the role of an 'enemy' fighter out to shoot down the unwary student. The basic aim of the exercise is simply to avoid being shot down (albeit in simulation), but the student is also expected to make 'track progression': 'The aim is not to turn off track and fight, but to run away, preferably towards the target. Then we include another ACM sortie, the Hawk being fitted with two AIM-nine Sidewinder missiles, to serve as an introduction to flying with missile armament. We can simulate either the Golf or Lima version of the Sidewinder, the Golf being a stern attack version, whereas the Lima has an all-round capability, and could be launched from any angle.'

The next part of the TWU course is the SAP phase, the Simulated Attack Profile: 'Again we build them up gently, with SAP One being flown dual, showing the student the fundamentals of bombing an off-range target, although naturally we don't actually carry bombs, and we don't fly below two hundred and fifty feet, being off range. After the dual they go off and fly the sortie as a pair, initially with the staff pilot leading, but then with the student in the lead. This works towards the final three SAPs where they will have a bounce aircraft thrown in too, and again the first of these sorties will be flown dual. In addition to the pressure of the bounce aircraft, we also pile on the pressure at the planning stage.'

Initially, the student will be given plenty of time to plan his route, normally around three hours, and he will be given two targets to locate. However, towards the end of the course the instructors will limit the planning time, giving the student the target locations two and a half hours before the take-off time, effectively giving him just one and a half hours to plan the sortie, thirty or forty minutes to brief it, and twenty minutes to get out to the aircraft and get airborne. Time over target is also introduced, so that the student not only has to locate and overfly the target, but reach the position within a few seconds of a time designated by the instructor.

The continual increase in pressure is designed gradually to improve the student's capabilities: 'All these little things build up, so that by the end of the course they are achieving a standard that they just wouldn't have thought possible at the beginning. But every individual skill is important. For example, with time-over-target tasks, you must remember that in an operational situation you may have a target that is the subject of a co-ordinated attack by other RAF squadrons or even other NATO forces. You may simply get a message to be over a specific target at a specific time, and have just a one-minute bracket to get in there and do the job. In the real world there could be four A-10s going in two minutes before you, and a recce Phantom running in afterwards, so the timing is very important. For us, we're not actually fighting a war, so it's purely a training asset, of course.' The TWU leads the students gently, slowly introducing different aspects of aerial warfare which become increasingly important as the students move towards the end of the TWU course, and a posting to a conversion unit, prior to joining an operational squadron.

Returning to air-to-air combat, the fledgling fighter pilots are taught to test their skills against an airborne banner, towed by one of the TWU Hawks: 'It's a sort of hessian flag, which we attach to one of our Hawks which has been modified for target-towing. The banner is towed at a distance of eight hundred feet from the Hawk, and the student goes off with a weapons instructor in the back seat, flying a second sortie with the cine camera, and then flying three hot sorties with ammunition in the gun. Judging how the student scores is relatively simple, as we tow the target back here, dropping it on the airfield near the runway, before bringing it back to the squadron for all to see. We paint the bullets with a coloured dye, with a different colour for each aircraft, and as the bullet goes through the target it leaves a coloured trace on the hessian. In this way we can put four or even six aircraft on the same target. Moving on, there's the advanced ACM phase, starting with a one-versus-one sortie using missile armament this time, as well as guns.' As with all of the earlier exercises, there is a set sequence of flights, building up from the first sortie.

Flying as a pair, the students aim to 'shoot down' a singleton: 'Two of these flights are flown dual, and if they perform okay they do the next flight solo. The fact that we do two flights dual in this case indicates that there is a great deal to teach them, with lots of safety aspects to consider when there are three aircraft in the same part of the sky. We then move on to a formation revision trip, and then the Air Defence phase, where we introduce them to practice intercepts, that is, the job that will really be their bread-and-butter on their front-line squadron. There's patently a great deal that we cannot teach them, as our Hawks don't have a radar, but we can give them the basics. We use a fairly close control from a nearby radar unit, starting with things like two-versus-one day-time intercepts, and ending-up with Capexes, launching two aircraft on a Combat Air Patrol in a given area, while another bounce aircraft tries to penetrate the CAP. Finally we have an Adex, an Air Defence Exercise, which is normally a simple Capex, but in this case we actually scramble the crew from the crewroom.' These final sorties are very hard work, navigating from one Combat Air Patrol area to another, all the time being threatened by the 'bounce' aircraft. The student has to make sure that he is not in danger of being shot down, and that the 'bounce' Hawk doesn't penetrate the CAP area, acting, as it does, as both an 'enemy' interceptor and bomber, by constantly changing modes as the circumstances dictate.

'For something like a medium-level practice intercept, we would fly as a pair under the control of a ground-based radar unit. This would be rather like being in a Tornado or Phantom with an unserviceable radar, having to rely entirely on directions from the radar controller on the ground. Alternatively we could fly under what we call Bravo Control, whereby there is a supply of radar information from the ground, but do our own control or direction. The basic information is the same, but in the latter situation the student has to decide what to do with the information. We would aim to manoeuvre the pair until we were in a position either to shoot down the intruder, or to perform a visual identification, as we don't automatically assume that the intruder is hostile.'

One of the instructing officers sets out the planned procedure: 'Air combat manoeuvres are taught right from the first exercise. On ACM One we try to concentrate on the offensive manoeuvres where the student has the upper hand, then on ACM Two we introduce the defensive moves where the student is being attacked. Moves include high yo-yos, low yo-yos, and rolling scissors, which isn't strictly an offensive move, but it's one that the Hawk tends to get into quite often. It's really a mutually defensive move, when you're both trying to avoid being shot down. A horizontal scissors is a low-speed move where the two aircraft are constantly turning in towards each other, crossing, and turning back towards each other again. The one who gets himself spat out in front of the other is the one who gets shot down, when the other guy gets his gunsight on to you. In most aircraft, horizontal scissors is quite common, but because of the Hawk's very good low-speed handling we often take the fight into the vertical. This is because you're effectively trying to arrest your forward progress, and a good way to do that is to barrel-roll around. Unfortunately the other guy will do the same thing, so we end up with the two aircraft in a kind of double spiral, with one aircraft on top while the other is on the bottom, while both pilots are trying to get behind each other. If you can't get behind the other guy, and you realise that you're starting to lose, it's important to realise this and run away, sooner rather than later. We try and fly two aircraft that are matched, performance-wise, but obviously if you put up one Hawk with pylons attached to the wings and another that is completely clean, the latter will win, with less drag and more lift at its disposal. However, the skill of the pilot is obviously a major factor.'

By the time that the students fly ACM Three or ACM Four, the instructors will have identified the good, the bad, and the average: 'The instructor will feed them situations, but the students vary dramatically. By this time you have identified some who are very good, maybe to a standard whereby the instructor just can't give him an inch. We're not going up there simply to shoot down the student, we're trying to bring out the best in him. But you do get some who take to ACM naturally, and others who have to work very hard to keep up. You have students with whom we have to fly a very hard ACM fight, and others who really have barely got a clue, and indeed, after their first solo attempt, you fell that they haven't got what it takes, and then we recommend that they go up for another dual flight.'

Safety is a very important aspect of air combat: 'We're very keen that the students must not break a minimum height of ten thousand feet, so we're talking about a height of two miles up, and that is the ground as far as we are concerned. The student must not be dangerous as regards collisions. There must be absolutely no risk that he's going to hit the other aeroplane. We have to be sure that he's not going to run out of fuel, and that he's going to handle the aeroplane and engine in a safe manner. The Hawk is a very forgiving machine. You can mishandle it to a great extent and it never bites you, whereas an aircraft like the Phantom most certainly will. The Hawk is an excellent trainer for the Tornado, which features almost foolproof handling as well. The Rolls Royce Adour engine in the Hawk is an incredibly reliable engine, but like any highly tuned unit, it works exceptionally well until you get to its limit, and then it will surge. An engine surge usually occurs because of mishandling the throttle, for instance, in a heavy buffet, turning behind somebody, accelerating the engine, and then hitting the slipstream of the aircraft in front of you. You disrupt the airflow into the intakes to such an extent that the compressor is literally gasping for breath, and too much fuel is flowing through, resulting in a surge. Normally you hear a bang or a loud popping, and certainly the gas turbine temperature dial will rise quite rapidly, but as long as you catch it quickly you can just close the throttle. If that doesn't cure it you have to stop-cock the engine and quickly perform a re-light. I must say that you don't get many instances like that, but you do train the students to be ready for it.

'We would wish that the aircraft didn't clock up a seven g count, for example, so we set the limit at six-point-nine. Seven wouldn't do the Hawk any damage, but it would use up fatigue life on the airframe. As for negative g, you would have to do some fairly exotic aerobatic manoeuvres to pull any, but the limit is three-point-five. I can't imagine anyone getting to even minus-two g, as we're really not in that sort of game, and we leave the outside loops and things like that to the Pitts Special stunt planes. Other things? Well, we wouldn't be impressed if anyone went into a spin during combat, not deliberately anyway. Chivenor is an ideal place for air combat, as we have virtually free airspace all around us, so we can get airborne and go where the weather is best. In combat you mustn't go into cloud or even go near it, so we need a block of airspace that is completely clear. Running away into cloud might be something you could do in a war, but it isn't something we encourage. Because of the cannon ammunition, ACM is normally flown over the sea, in an area that is confirmed as being clear. For the ground-attack students, the off-range targets are always pre-determined features that have been approved, such as bridges, electrical sub-stations, transmission towers, industrial buildings and so on. Certainly they are never private houses. We prefer to have a number of pre-determined targets, but the routes are not normally pre-planned, and we let the students plan their own routes, which is much more valuable for training purposes. They plan it and they have got to live with it, and it does mean that the routes do vary, and nobody has to live with a steady stream of aircraft racing over his house all day.

'We run a very traditional system of assessment here. The rest of the air force has largely gone over to a system approach with objectives, aims and all sorts of things. The net result is that they end up with write-up forms where you have to assess what the guy knew, what he needed to know, did he do this or that, and all finishing with ticks in boxes. I'm totally biased, I'll admit, but what that achieves is mediocrity. In that system the guys don't have to excel, they merely have to be good enough, and that doesn't exactly encourage you. Here at Chivenor, each sortie is written up by the instructor, and it's purely his assessment that is written down. The length of the write-up will probably depend on how well the student did. If he did well, a couple of sentences will normally suffice. We do give the student a mark from zero to three, with zero being a fail, and a three being something just short of God. So you don't often get a three, and we can amplify the score with a plus or a minus, and the average sortie tends to be a score of two. The scores will be there on the wall for all to see, so we've introduced an element of competition, and the students can take the piss out of each other when they see how they have performed. The write-up is confidential, however, and although they will obviously be thoroughly debriefed after each sortie, they are not encouraged to read the write-ups, even though they can if they want to. They might get the wrong impression if they did, as what tends to get written down are the bad points only. There's little point in writing that the guy did okay, as we don't need to take any action on that kind of performance. However, we don't lock up the books, and human nature being what it is . . .

'By encouraging the students to read their reports, I doubt if you would have such an honest system, because we would then write them in the knowledge that the students are going to read them, and so we might be tempted to pull a few punches. I prefer the system we have got now, writing exactly what we think, with an honest debrief, and if he still wants to read his report, we let him. You see, the guy might be a complete wanker, but you would be reluctant to put that on the write-up. You have to be honest but constructive as well. At the end of the day, the student will end up with a couple of folders. One will contain all the sortie write-ups, and the other the weaponry, with results of all his weapons sorties. By using that information we will write an end-of-course report on him, which is broken down into phases, such as ground school, simulator, right through all the flying phases, ending with a summary by the Flight Commander and Squadron Commander, plus the Officer Commanding Flying, and finally the Group Captain who will add his literary pearls to it. The Flight Commander will be the one who has the most contact with the student, and he will run his course in effect, but the Squadron Commander will know him quite well too. The Wing Commander will probably have flown at least one or two sorties with the student, and what he is really doing is adding his experience to point out any particular areas which he feels are significant.

'The net result is that we end up with three or four bits of paper that will act as a permanent record as to how he did here at the TWU at Chivenor. They will be sent to his next unit, his OCU, the Operational Conversion Unit, where the documents will be used as a guide by his new instructors, as they teach him to operate a front-line fighter. We try to be totally fair, as we're certainly not out to nail anyone. We try desperately hard to get them to succeed and pass them out. They have already cost the RAF a great deal of money, so the last thing we would want to do is to chop someone at this late stage. But on the other hand we have to remember that people's lives are at stake here, not only the student's own, but other crews', and maybe those of people on the ground, too. We don't go out of our way to create tension, and we wouldn't want every day to be like a driving test for the student. Every sortie *is* a test, in that they can pass or fail each one, but the aim of the game is to relax the guy as much as possible, as naturally we want to see him at his best. If we really wanted to, we could have a guy in tears before he even walked out to his aircraft, but obviously we wouldn't be achieving very much by doing that.

'At the end of the TWU course we will have a role dispersal meeting, where we get together with the postings people, and we work out a mutually acceptable agreement as to which student goes where. The postings guys will come along with the number of slots that are currently available, maybe four Tornado GR1 slots, two or three Tornado F3 slots, a couple of Phantoms and one Harrier for example. We might not have enough students to fill all the slots, but we will have a very good idea of which students will be best suited to each slot. Most guys do inevitably want to go to a single-seater, be it the Harrier or Jaguar, much of this being a natural degree of bravado I suspect, but they are all more than happy to go on to the Tornado or Buccaneer. Some will desperately want to go on to fighters, either Tornado or Phantom, and we have their measure of ability, the postings guys have the slots, and so we endeavour to put round pegs into round holes where we can.

'Typically a student will have to wait something like six to eight weeks before joining his OCU, and after finishing here he will probably want some leave in any case, and precise times do vary. If we can't start him at an OCU within about ten weeks of completing his TWU course here, we will bring him back to do a refresher course of about five hours, just to get him back into the swing of things again, as we do want him to be as well equipped as possible when the arrives at his OCU. We don't want to send guys there who will not make it, because the further through training you go, the more expensive it is when someone fails. People do fail, and sadly we do get guys who are chopped from the squadrons, and when a guy has cost you over three million pounds you really don't want to chop him; but if the guy just cannot hack the job, or if safety is involved, you really have no other option. In many respects their hardest work will be done here at Chivenor, because whatever aircraft they may go to from here, it will have more advanced systems, things like inertial navigation . . . possibly not very reliable equipment in some cases, but something to hang their hat on. For instance, when we get people coming back here from the Tornado to join our staff, they have to work very hard to get back up to speed, because here they have no moving map in the cockpit to tell them where they are, or a navigator in the back seat whispering in their ear. Here they are back navigating by purely looking out of the window.

'Aside from the actual flying training itself, life here is much the same as it was for them at Valley. We do expect them to act as big boys now, as they are out of Support Command, and they are expected to behave accordingly without any additional training on our part. They do perform Duty Officer activities here, looking after basic day-to-day matters, but most of the time here at Chivenor is really centred on the flying. They are almost encouraged to wear their flying kit most of the time, and we do try to develop a kind of social rapport between student and instructor. They are always told what is going on, and they are invited to squadron dinners and things like that. In every respect we just try to get them used to how things will be when they join a front-line squadron.'

7

CONVERSION

Having left the Tactical Weapons Unit, the student pilot now goes on an OCU — an Operational Conversion Unit, where he will learn to fly and fight with the aircraft types flown by the Royal Air Force's front-line fighter/ bomber squadrons. For the prospective fighter pilot, this means a posting to the Tornado Operational Conversion Unit (229 OCU), which doubles as No. 65 Reserve Squadron, at RAF Coningsby in Lincolnshire.

'Depending on their respective backgrounds, we basically have three different groups of arrivals here at 229 OCU. Firstly we have the straight-through guys, those that have done basic and advanced flying training and then a Tactical Weapons Unit, before coming here. Then there are those who are former Phantom or Lightning pilots who have been away on Staff jobs within the RAF on non-flying duties, and after returning to the Tactical Weapons Unit, they come here to re-train on Tornado.

Finally we have the guys who are coming straight from the F-4 squadrons, to be converted on to the Tornado. They are all ex-air defenders, however, as we don't cross-role and take former "mud-movers" as that would be too complicated. So there are three basic groups for which we run a Long Course and a Short Course which run concurrently. They are both essentially the same course but with bits taken out or added accordingly.'

The OCU Qualified Flying Instructor continues: 'When they come here they will already have been to RAF Mountbatten, where they will have done some combat survival and rescue training with the kit that they will use in the aeroplane, and that takes about three or four days. Then they will spend a few more days at the Aero-medical Centre at North Luffenham where they'll again get used to the kit and so on. If they are new students who have never really operated air defence interceptors before, they will get here a couple of weeks early ahead of the course, and do what we call a Radar Lead-in, using Micro Air Intercept Trainers, and just learning the basics of the air picture of intercepts; and they will need the two weeks just to get hold of the basic concepts. What they will have is a B-scope, on the bottom of which you have what is effectively your position. So if a target is coming towards you, it doesn't just run down the radar picture, it'll shoot off sharply to one side or the other at the last minute, if it isn't actually going to hit you. So they'll spend two weeks getting the idea of that, on lectures and on the Micro AIT. If they are former air defence pilots they obviously wouldn't need to do that, and they will join at the Ground School phase which lasts for four weeks, learning the aircraft systems, be they hydraulics, electrics, fuel, fly-by-wire, or whatever. You have the computer system, the TV tabulator system, radar, although nothing too detailed on the radar, as they'll come to that later.

'The Ground School is tied in with CEPT, that's Cockpit Emergency Procedure Trainer, these being static simulators which don't do anything apart from reacting to the right switches, so they're not mobile, full-motion simulators. However, towards the end of the Ground School they will start using the mission simulator, with no visual or actual motion, but on this they can learn procedures for departure, landing and the various crew procedures, because some of the students will not have flown with a navigator in the second seat before, or at least, will not have flown very often with a navigator, and so they need to learn crew co-operation. Certainly when they start here, a specific pilot will be placed with a specific navigator, but this is only an administrative convenience, in that we will try to put a straight-through pilot with a straight-through navigator, and a former F-4 pilot and navigator together, and so on, as this helps with the running of the course, but it doesn't mean they will stay together all the time. They will tend to, unless there are problems. On the squadrons they try to run a constituted crew system, whereby a pilot will have his own navigator and vice versa, but there are disadvantages with this. For example, you will find that maybe a third of the crews are superb, and they all get on well together, a third will be okay, nothing fantastic, and another third of the crews will hate each other, and clearly you can't work like that. There's consequently nothing to stop us changing crews around if we want to.

'Still with simulators, while they are learning the procedures and becoming more confident, we will start feeding in emergencies, which they have to deal with on top of flying the aeroplane, which in an aeroplane such as the Tornado can be very complicated. On Simulator Seven exercise, a Qualified Flying Instructor will sit in on the exercise, as at this stage we will allocate a QFI to a specific crew, and he'll get an idea of what it will be like to fly with this crew before they actually start flying. He'll be able to see how they are, whether a guy is really sharp, enthusiastic, whether he gets confused or panics easily, and so on.'

With the ground training completed, the OCU course continues in the air: 'Basically the course is divided into four phases, starting with the Conversion Phase, which is purely teaching the pilot to fly the Tornado from all points of view, from straight and level, low level, instrument flying, combat manoeuvring, turning upside down, night flying, close formation, battle formation, the whole thing, taking twelve sorties. On his first sortie he'll fly dual in a twin-control aircraft with a QFI in the rear seat, and simply get the feel of the aeroplane, what it's like going fast, going slow, with the wings forward, the wings swept back, how it turns, and so on. At the same time, his navigator partner does a similar Convex, learning more about his own environment, working his computers, using all the kit, just general familiarisation. On the pilot's Convex Three, he'll be shown how fast the Tornado will go, with a reheat climb that will take about a minute from brakes-off to being five miles high, levelling off there, going supersonic, to see what handling is like at that speed, then a look at degraded performance, flying without the fly-by-wire system using mechanical control. Then he'll come back here to do some circuits and bumps, as we want to get them confident at landing and taking-off.'

The training continues, and more of the Tornado F3's capabilities are gradually introduced to the student pilot: 'On Convex Four we demonstrate single engine operation, how to fly at low level over land and over the sea, a little aerobatics, maximum rate turning, high angle-of-attack manoeuvring, which is a very slow dogfight kind of flying. Then back for some more circuits. If at that stage we think he's okay and he can land safely, we'll send him solo, that is, with a staff navigator in the back seat, and the pilot will fly his first solo, involving medium-level flying, a low-level navigation exercise, maybe forty minutes at two hundred and fifty feet and four hundred knots, medium- or high-level transit back here, some general handling out over the sea, then back for a few circuits. Then he does a crew solo with his navigator, and does virtually the same thing again. Having covered the general flying we go on to instrument flying. Tornado is such an easy aircraft to fly, the instrumentation is so good, it doesn't take them long to learn, and by the time they get to this stage they are pretty familiar with instruments in any case, having used them all through the course. Then on Convex Eight we have close formation, leading, and being number two, and flying battle formation, or tactical positioning, at medium level and right down to two hundred and fifty feet over the sea. The sortie is flown as a two-aircraft formation.' On operational sorties, fighter pilots will normally operate as pairs for mutual defence, keeping a careful eye on each other's vital 'six-o'clock' position. For practice purposes it is obviously necessary for someone to play the 'bad guy', so that the fighter pilot has a target to fly his interception against.

However, the 'ideal package' is a four-aircraft formation: 'The ability of the Tornado to intercept and track-while-scan a lot of targets means that we can be very flexible in air combat. You never fight fair in air defence. You never accept a one-on-one fight, so if there's three of them and two of you, you run away. Or maybe you try to make sure they don't know you're there, and you creep up on them . . . it's not a polite game. So while you might sometimes fly as a singleton, on your own holding Combat Air Patrol, going after whatever target you're directed to, generally you would fly as a pair or two pairs, if you can. Consequently we would fly a four-ship on occasion.

'So the students will fly a practice as a pair, at medium and low level, then a tail-chase, the first part of learning to handle the weapons, and you're manoeuvring the aircraft in conjunction with another one. It's the beginning of dogfighting. They then fly a pairs approach and landing. If the crew is what we call a re-tread, former Phantom or Lightning pilots, that's all they will get on the formation side. If they are new straight-through students they will do another sortie where the guy who was leading now becomes number two. There is as much of an art, or skill, in leading a formation as in being number two, as the latter is a sort of motor reaction of the leader, so the leader has constantly to think outside, for his wingman. Then they do some night flying, back with a QFI, mainly working with instruments, learning to haul the machine round on instruments at low level, at night, and they really work hard on that . . . they earn their money. Then we teach them to fly the circuit at night, and if they do that well enough they go off and do all that with their navigator in the back seat. Then they take their instrument Rating Test. If they are the basic straight-through students they go on to Convex Thirteen, the navigator's first real look at this formation flying. They'll go off with a QFI and student pilot in one aircraft, and a Staff pilot and student navigator in the other, to a bit of close formation, battle formation, some tail-chasing, so that the navigator can get the aspects of the tail-chase on his radar, tucked in behind the other aircraft. Then a look at the radar as they split out at about thirty miles, turn and point at each other, and find each other on radar. Then after another split the navigator will be given more tasks like putting in the information for a diversion to an airfield somewhere, basically making sure that he knows his kit. After that we're at the end of the Convex phase.'

There follows a further two days of ground-based lectures on the missile systems and the radar before moving on to the second part of the OCU course, the Basic Radar Phase: 'Perhaps it would be better called the Basic Intercept Phase. They'll get airborne, go out about a hundred and fifty miles over the North Sea to get away from the airways and all the other traffic, and at fifteen thousand feet or above they will split by fifty miles, and one guy runs in while the other learns how to pick him up on radar, understanding the geometry of how to put your aircraft in the right place. We normally operate on an attack, re-attack basis, where if the target is judged to be hostile, the pilot will fire head-on a Sky Flash missile when he's up to about fifteen miles, but assuming that it will miss the target he then does a re-attack, coming around the target to fire off a Sidewinder heat-seeking missile from the rear. The pilot will be taught the rudiments of doing the intercept, although it's the navigator who is the tactical commander and he really controls the attack. Every sortie is preceded by a TAIT exercise, on the Tornado Airborne Intercept Trainer. (It should really be called the Tornado Intercept Trainer, but we couldn't call it the TIT! However, it's another mission simulator.) So they will start off flying one-versus-one without flying any evasion manoeuvres. Then one-versus-one with evasion, with the target aircraft trying not to be caught, but within limitations, nothing really serious. We then move down to low level and do the same thing with the target at two hundred and fifty feet, so that they're using the radar in a look-down mode.

'Just when the student thinks everything is wonderful, we throw in two targets, doing the same thing at medium level, one-versus-two so you've got to shoot both of them down, working out your tactics, then one-versus-two with evasion, then the same thing down at low level. Each sortie is assessed, and although it's a teaching sortie they do have to reach a set standard. If they fall below that standard they will fly the same sortie again, and if they still fall below the required standard they are put on Review, and we give them what we call a package. We'll look at the guy and identify in what areas he is weak, and then concentrate on these aspects, giving him a few sorties to bring him up to par again. If he still doesn't come up to scratch then he has to go, and he's sent off somewhere else. This is one of the most highly qualified jobs for both a pilot and navigator. So if somebody doesn't make it here, he might well go on to the Tornado GR1, or maybe on to the Canberra squadrons, depending on his abilities and the RAF's requirements. It may be that he's just better suited to the mud-moving world rather than air defence.'

Next comes the Combat Phase. The students will first be re-familiarised with some of the handling aspects explored earlier in the OCU course: 'We will remind them of some of the things they've already seen, the heavy manoeuvring, the high-g or low speed and high angle-of-attack combat manoeuvring, learning how to get the best out of the aeroplane. They will then fly with a QWI, a Qualified Weapons Instructor, who will show the students the tactical applications of what they have already learned. The first Combat Phase exercise is also a mid-course handling check. We find that the students have been taught how to handle the aeroplane, fly the circuit, land, go off on radar sorties, come back having used all their fuel, as we never come back with loads of fuel, we use every bit and come back with just the minimum safe amount in the tanks, so the guys rarely have enough fuel to do any circuits at this stage. So we find that they go off and do combat flying, rush around with their hair on fire, and come back short of fuel, screw-up the circuit, and get into a panic. So apart from teaching the rudiments of combat, we check at this stage that they still know how to fly the aeroplane properly. If we see any weakness we will correct it.

'As for the kind of moves we will then teach them, we will initially look at what happens if they get a nose-high attitude, with the speed getting very low. In certain circumstances you could do what is known as a loaded pull back on the guy who is attacking you, but if the speed gets really low, well you're probably going to die in combat anyway. We'll look at high angle-of-attack manoeuvring, that's the scissors, flat scissors and rolling scissors. Now, obviously you can't teach a guy that sort of thing without a second aeroplane, but at this stage we teach him the basic handling techniques by bringing him down to low speed, teaching him how to use his angle of attack, when to use reheat and so on. At this low speed you won't be pulling much g-force at all, but it certainly isn't in any way genteel, as everything is buffeting and vibrating and you're working quite hard. You're flying at a speed of around two hundred to two hundred and fifty knots and about nineteen units of angle of attack, which is very high. You're basically sitting on your power and the SPILS, the Spin Prevention and Incidence Limitation System, will prevent you automatically from using too much control column which would cause you to go into a spin, so you're then slightly un-loading the aircraft, and learning a feel for that sort of handling. There's really only about two g involved.

'They will also look at maximum rate turning, a fighter pilot's bread and butter; how to get the maximum performance in the horizontal, vertical or oblique planes. You don't bother with the sixty-seven degrees wing setting, as that's essentially a go-faster position, a run-away wing, an attack-at-high-speed wing. So you'll turn with a forty-five degrees wing setting, with six to seven g, and that's quite severe, more than even the spacemen ever used, although not quite as much as the F-16 for example, which can pull about nine g, but then Tornado is an interceptor, not an air superiority fighter. Then we'll try the same turn but without as much energy, which is a situation you might find yourself in, so we'll try a twenty-five degrees wing, and about two hundred and ninety knots, which comes out at about four and a half g. If you're in that low-energy situation we then look at the bug-out, basically reducing all of the drag on the airframe, un-loading the turn, getting your speed back as quickly as possible, and then you either want to run away because you don't like what you see, or you're getting energy back before you pitch back into the fight again. Having done all that on the sortie, we then give them a simulated emergency, come back here and look at their circuit flying, and then the QWI will go through almost the same thing again, but this time looking at tactical applications rather than the handling.

'On the next sortie we fly with the student navigator and staff pilot, together with the QWI and student pilot, flying their two aircraft respectively; and they'll practise the various manoeuvres, for example the high yo-yo, pulling up from the turn, the low yo-yo, losing height, then pulling up back into the turn, and then a lesson in how you often don't need that kind of manoeuvre in this aircraft as it can almost turn square corners. If you're fighting a Phantom you don't have much of a problem, but with two aircraft of similar performance as in this situation, or if you're up against something like the F-15, you might have to employ moves like that to gain an advantage. They will look at flat and rolling scissors on the next sortie, and then they will start what we call neutral splits, using the radar. So they'll split at about forty miles, come in towards each other, ideally supersonic, and then try to get the head-on missiles, the Sky Flash, off against each other; and then as they cross on the merge, go into the close-in dogfighting. Although if we were doing this for real, we teach them that they should fire off their missiles and just blow through and disappear, if they don't like what they see. He who turns and runs away, lives to fight another day.

'Eventually they will reach a stage where they can fly dissimilar air combat, flying two-versus-two or two-versus-four, often against Hawks, when we get a detachment from one of the TWUs. Although the Hawks aren't supersonic they are very capable little fighters and they will come over to Coningsby and act as our targets. So a Tornado can take on two Hawks, head-on, combat and so on. The Hawks don't have radar, but they are given control by the ground-based radar stations, whereas the Tornado crew won't be given that information so they have to use the aircraft's radar. Then two-versus-two, then two-versus-four. This will be against Hawks, F-16s, or indeed anybody we can find . . . we never have enough targets. And that's the Combat phase completed.'

The final stage in the OCU course is the Advanced Radar phase, starting at the point where the Basic phase left off. At this stage the students rapidly progress to two-versus-four radar intercepts at any height, using evasion, flying overland and supersonic intercepts, sometimes at heights in excess of 40,000 feet, or as little as 250 feet, during low level overland exercises. At the very end of this phase the students will be given what is referred to as a 'Tac Check', where they will be required to organise a number of airborne targets, contacting the Harrier, Jaguar or Tornado squadrons (or indeed any willing participants), and then planning a sortie over land or over sea, briefing it, and leading it. At least two of the four-ship formation they will lead will be flown by Staff crews, in order that the entire operation can be monitored and assessed thoroughly. The sortie is debriefed on video with voice recording: 'Nobody can tell a lie, as everything is recorded. With that exercise completed, that's the end of the OCU course. It will last between four and five months.

'Ninety-five per cent of our students get through the course successfully. Some do have difficulties, but not those that I call the Space-Invaders types who have come straight through the training system. We've had trouble with former Phantom navigators, as they can find it hard to convert to the computer-driven kit that we have. But the loss rate is low. We might chop one navigator on every two courses or so; with pilots, even fewer. The Tornado is not difficult to fly; but because it's so easy, a great deal more is required of you on the tactical and leadership side of things.

'Having finished the OCU course, the training isn't over, because they go to their first squadron and go through a squadron work-up period, which normally lasts between three and six months, and only then can they be declared as being Limited Operational. It's going to be another three months before they are fully operational. When they leave here they are regarded as being Limited Combat Ready, a Nato standard, but the RAF requirement is much higher, so they go over to their squadron and train still further. After about three months on the unit they will be termed as Limited Operational which is the RAF Strike Command-designated status, which means they can now start to hold QRA, Quick Reaction Alert. It's only in the fullness of time that they will be trained sufficiently to be classed as Fully Operational, and then they can be let loose, to lead four-ships and so on. Having come to us from the Tactical Weapons Units, they have already formed a kind of attitude, in that they will have flown as fighter pilots in the historical sense, rushing around with Hawks one-versus-one and so on. When they get here, it can be a bit of a shock in that things are not quite how they expected: the old image of the fighter pilot just doesn't apply in the 'nineties, the technology is so different. It's a long time from leaving the TWU to becoming fully operational on a squadron. About a year in fact. There is a great deal to learn.

'I'm a great fan of the Tornado. The United Kingdom

Air Defence Region is the largest region in Nato. If you drew a line from Iceland to Norway and then about a hundred miles around Ireland, all the way down to the Bay of Biscay, and halfway across the English Channel, then everything within that is the UK Air Defence Region. So what do you want from an aircraft that has to defend that kind of area? You want an aeroplane that has very long range. You want an aeroplane that can detect at very long range, looking up and looking down, coping with lots of targets. You want an aeroplane that can carry lots of weapons. The only aspect of the Tornado which even slightly fails to meet these criteria is that the radar doesn't see quite as far as the manufacturer said it would, but having said that, its range is more than adequate. It's all I need. For instance, if I can't intercept a target after picking it up on radar at, say, fifty miles, then there's something wrong with me. If he's approaching me super-sonic, then maybe I'd need about seventy miles, but in that situation the target would normally be flying fairly high, and our ground radars would pick him up and vector me on to him. It was never designed to be an air superiority fighter, so, for example, I wouldn't want to mix it with a Fulcrum or an F-15, but at the same time I would fight with them more happily than I would have done with a Phantom. From the point of view of its manoeuvrability, at low level it is very good; its turning rate is very close to that of an F-15, up to about ten thousand feet or so. It is the fastest aeroplane around. It will be cleared to eight hundred and fifty knots, and you have to throttle back at seven hundred and fifty knots, so that's very, very fast. There's absolutely nothing that can run away from us.

'Supersonic at high level, it is also very good. Every-body waxes lyrical about the Lightning; well, I flew Light-nings, and the Tornado will fly just as fast, and having gone that fast, and manoeuvred just as hard, it will have more fuel, and what's more, it carries eight weapons. Where it is possibly weak is at a medium level at lower speeds, and at high levels at lower speed. Although it is a swing-wing design, it doesn't have enough wing basically, until you go supersonic with the wings swept back, when it's like a Lightning. It's disappointing in heavy manoeuvring at medium and high level until you get supersonic. The stuff you read about fatigue is absolute rubbish. Okay, some aircraft have been put into storage, but they were early model F2s, all of which have plenty of fatigue life, and the plan has always been to update them to F2A standard, with all the equipment of the later F3, but with the earlier, less powerful engine, and then reissue them to us at the OCU. However, because we were expected to lose some aircraft with an attrition rate of about ten per cent, we haven't got the F2As back here, because we simply don't need them. We've only lost one Tornado F3 since we began flying the type in 1985, so we've got them coming out of our ears in effect. It's got nothing to do with pulling the wings off at all, we just have no requirement for them as yet. Sure, there is a fatigue programme like there is for the Phantom. Like any aeroplane, you wouldn't want the whole fleet, which entered service at the same time, to be put into long-term servicing at the same time, for strengthening and so on. So with a fatigue index line we can identify when, for example, a particular aeroplane might be a little high on fatigue, so we can avoid flying it on the higher fatigue kind of exercises. So by carefully monitoring the fatigue lives we can ensure that all the aircraft go away for servicing at different times.

'We designed the course so that there are specific sorties where the pilot doesn't need to pull g. We then say that he doesn't need to pull g at that stage; so don't pull it gratuitously, you go around the corner sensibly. But then there are other sorties — combat sorties for example — where you can just about pull the wings off and use the aeroplane literally as it was designed to be used. Okay, it's not as beefy, as tough as it should be, but it was originally designed as a ground-attack aircraft which doesn't really use much fatigue life.

'The radar is somewhat behind the most recent radar technology, but contrary to popular rumour we don't have concrete in any of our radomes. I've been on the

OCU since it started flying Tornado, and the aircraft didn't have concrete in the noses even then. That tale came purely from the days when the aircraft at Warton did fly with concrete ballast, while RAF guys were simply learning how to fly them. Okay, over the years one or two aircraft might have had ballast fitted to enable us to fly an aircraft on a sortie where radar wasn't required, while its radar might have been unserviceable, that's all. The tales in the newspapers were completely untrue. Originally the Tornado F3's radar was very poor, but we accepted it on the basis that it was only ever an interim radar. The squadrons now have a good radar and it's quite a viable proposition. We've got American, Canadian, Australian, Norwegian and French exchange officers here, and none of them has commented that the radar is in any way inferior.

'It just depends on what you want. The Tornado is much better suited to my job than a F-16 for example. I wouldn't want to be a hundred and fifty miles out over the North Sea on my own in an F-16. Its radar is very limited in range. I'm certainly a Tornado fan. I saw the Lightning at the very beginning, I saw the Mirage at its beginning in air defence, and I saw the Phantom at the start of its air defence operations, so I've seen teeth-cutting exercises before, and while the Tornado F3's entry into service did suffer more than its fair share of problems, we now have an aircraft that we're very happy with. It isn't perfect, but you can never have the best of everything. If you were to ask the guys if they would rather go to war in this or a Phantom, they would pick the Tornado. It hasn't got some things which other fighters have, like chaff and flare dispensers and so on, but we will get them. It sounds like an optimistic view, but I don't think I've overstated the case. I have over a thousand hours on the type, two thousand on the Phantom and five hundred on the Mirage, a thousand on the Lightning, and I've flown the Meteor, Vampire and F-104, so I've been around. I've flown in the F/A-18 too, and okay, it's very nice, thank you, but to go the same distance and do the same sorties that we do, flying clean without

Above: Groundcrew paying careful attention to a Tornado F3, above and below the exhausts of the two RB-199 turbofans.

Below: Groundcrew in full NBC warfare suits, guarding a Phantom of No. 56 Squadron outside its HAS (Hardened Aircraft Shelter) during an exercise.

Left: The pilot's view of a refuelling basket trailing behind a Hercules tanker over Cornwall. The Hercules is capable of transferring fuel to almost every RAF type equipped with a probe.

Below: A Buccaneer, armed with anti-shipping missiles, with its refuelling probe safely plugged into a tanker's basket.

Above: The RAF maintains two squadrons of SAR (Search and Rescue) Sea King and Wessex helicopters, tasked with the recovery of downed airmen. Here, a Sea King swoops into action.

Below: A Phantom FGR2 from No. 228 OCU (Operational Conversion Unit), which doubled as No. 64 Reserve Squadron until early 1991, when the OCU was disbanded and a smaller training flight formed at RAF Wattisham.

Pilot and navigator beside their Tornado F3 on the OCU
flight line at RAF Coningsby.

external fuel tanks, the Hornet would have to wear a belly tank which would reduce its performance, and in that situation it's not such a fancy mover. It's a case of horses for courses. With the Tornado F3 you could get airborne with tanks, refuel off Manston, and go all the way to Cyprus. It's wonderful, and although it flies like a lead balloon with huge tanks under the wings, it has a huge range.'

Another QFI at OCU continues: 'The Tornado is a very straightforward aircraft to fly, it's rather like a big Hawk, and unlike the Phantom which has the aerodynamics of a brick, the Tornado has the aid of computers, things like SPILS, which will minimise the risk of over-handling the aircraft, causing it to depart from normal flight. You will move the controls, demanding an input, and the computer will effectively tell you what you can and cannot safely do, depending on the flight conditions you happen to be in. A nice and easy machine to fly, very comfortable, and it has no vices, at least nothing that we've discovered yet, and we've been flying the Tornado for a long time.'

8

THE FRONT LINE

After years of intensive training, the aspiring fighter pilot completes the Operational Conversion course, and is posted to his first front-line RAF air defence squadron. For the Tornado pilots this means a move to one of three bases: Leuchars in Scotland (43 and 111 Squadrons), Leeming in Yorkshire (11, 23 and 25 Squadrons) or Coningsby, where Nos. 5 and 29 Squadrons share the airfield facilities with the OCU. Phantom pilots, no longer first-tour OCU graduates, are now drawn from a training flight at Wattisham, where they join either Nos. 56 or 74 Squadron, or one of two RAF Germany Squadrons, Nos. 19 and 92 at Wildenrath.

'The first trip a pilot gets with his squadron is with a Squadron QFI in the back seat. We need to know if the guy can fly the aeroplane, and if he can fly our aircraft, more specifically. This is split into two parts, a sort of area familiarisation and a handling check, plus a third flight if it's needed.' In the noisy confines of No. 74 Squadron's Operations Room, a Phantom pilot describes how the new arrival will slowly familiarise himself with life on the 'front line': 'Our Phantom is slightly different to the aircraft that the Phantom students will have flown at Leuchars. Apart from cockpit-layout switch positions, the engines on our Phantom, the F-4J, are totally different, so read-out captions and emergency procedures have to be changed accordingly. We like to think that our Phantoms are a little bit slicker than most, as our aircraft has a slightly narrower fuselage, due to the engine's dimensions being smaller than the Rolls Royce engines in the rest of the RAF Phantom fleet. The other Phantoms are probably the heaviest and most expensive ones built, but at the same time they're the most powerful. Ours have the American J-79-10B with a little less thrust, but there's no real noticeable change in performance, and at high level we have what is essentially a pure jet engine. So all the air that goes through the intake comes out of the engine's exhaust; whereas on the Rolls Royce Spey, some of the intake air flows around the engine . . . so our aircraft tend to perform better at high level. However, apart from one extra sortie because of the differences between our aircraft and all the other RAF Phantoms, our conversion course is exactly the same as for all the other squadrons, as laid down by No. 11 Group. After the initial familiarisation, there are two sorties at medium level, these being split so that you have a baby pilot with a combat-ready navigator, and a baby navigator with a combat-ready pilot, just to check them out and make sure they're doing everything correctly. These are just basic interception exercises, to settle them down.

'Then off we go with the Supersonic phase, launching as a pair, and one will be the target, the other acting as interceptor; then swapping over. Normally as a high speed target you would be up at about thirty thousand feet doing a speed in excess of Mach one point two. On the high-flyer exercise you again go off as a pair, flying as target and interceptor in turn, and you'll be up above forty thousand feet at about point nine or one point one

Mach. The thinner the air the more different there is in the intercept geometry. You have to fly progressively wider turns.

'Then there's the Tanking phase, and although the main blocks of the course are run in order, you don't have to fly each individual exercise in chronological sequence. You can chop and change, but some things *do* have to run in order, such as the first supersonic exercise in the simulator. Obviously you could have maybe ten goes at it in the simulator, until you solve all the minor glitches you might have, before you go out and fly it in the aircraft. With the tanking phase the navigator does come along, but it's essentially a pilot phase. Air-to-air refuelling comes with practice . . . it's rather like riding a bicycle. On a refuelling sortie we would actually take on fuel from the tanker — apart from performing a series of what we call "dry" prods, where we're just lining-up and aiming at the refuelling basket with our probe. As I say, it's like riding a bike — in that when you know *how* to do it, you don't know *why* you know how, you just do; and everything starts to look right and the probe goes into the basket, or it doesn't. Simple as that. Normally when a baby pilot goes up there, the first time he success-fully makes contact he will take on fuel, as that might be the last time he gets it into the basket, and after that he'll just practise dry prodding.

'Sometimes we get the Hercules tanker, a single-point refueller, and sometimes we get the Victor, with a hose trailing from either wing or from the centre under the fuselage. So in that case you have a choice of three bas-kets, and although the fuel flow rate is different for the wing or fuselage hoses, the Phantom can take fuel faster than any of the tankers can give it out, so there is no problem. We prefer the centre-line as fuel comes in much faster that way. The most common tanker is the VC10, another three point refueller, but the Victor is becoming pretty rare now. And also we get the Tristar with two centre hoses, and we have to practise refuelling with all those types. If you ask maybe six pilots how you perform a refuelling, you'll probably get six different answers. For instance I don't actually use the alignment markings that are painted under the tanker. Somebody will tell you one technique and you'll have a go, not have much success, so you'll try another. I move up and position myself in a waiting position about six feet back from the basket. Then I get the vertical and horizontal positioning sorted out until it looks about right, and then move the throttles forward a little bit to get me moving forward, and I either plug in, or miss. That's about all the advice I could give, and if it doesn't work, you have to back off and start again.

'After that we'll move on and try silent tanking without any radio communication, which is an important skill for a wartime operation where obviously you wouldn't want any RT chatter to give your position away. So you join on the tanker's port wing and put out the refuelling probe. You then go round behind and follow the set of indicator lights that are under the tanker, telling you when to refuel, when fuel is flowing and so on. By this stage you're getting pretty good at it as you'll have done about ten attempts. Then you try heavyweight, either with the three external tanks fitted, or you take the tanker up another five thousand feet, which has the same effect on the Phantom's performance. In that situation you have to refuel with one engine in reheat; because, as the fuel comes in, the weight goes up and you need more power to keep you at the same speed behind the tanker. So you come out of the basket, select afterburner for one engine and plug back in again. After that there's night tanking which is certainly interesting, not least because the basket isn't lit, so you have to follow the hose down visually from the tanker until you find it, and you also have to fly a silent tanking at night . . . all very hard work.

'Then we're on to the ACT phase, the Air Combat Training. We have a one-versus-one duel, which is really a pilot-handling check, throwing the aircraft about doing various things. When you're flying with a high angle-of-attack you have to handle the aircraft differently. We say that when it buffets, use your boot. When you're in this kind of situation, the aircraft will shake around quite heavily, and you fly various manoeuvres like rudder reversals, rolling and turning the aircraft by using the rudder instead of the ailerons, which wouldn't have much effect in these conditions. Also we do stalls and various other handling exercises like that. After that you can go on to low-level visual evasion, down to two hundred and fifty feet. Then Electronic Counter Measures work, four sorties, two in the simulator and two in the air with either one or two targets, working with 360 Squadron's ECM Canberras. They will use their electronic jamming equipment to try and stop our radars from functioning properly, and we try all of our methods of trying to intercept our target while all that is going on.

'Then a Low-Level phase which for us means anything below five thousand feet, flying a couple of ARAs and a couple of sterns. An ARA is an Attack-Re-Attack, firing a head-on missile such as Sky Flash, then you break away and come around to the back of the target, and fire off a rear attack missile such as the Sidewinder. A stern attack is a less aggressive manoeuvre where you sneak around to his six-o'clock and have a look at the target, see what it is and so on. This is the kind of intercept we would fly against a Soviet Bear over the North Sea. You wouldn't want to go into an intercept like that aggressively when we're at peace, so we approach from the back and come up gently and take a look, see what he's doing, taking pictures or whatever. All these low-level exercises are one-versus-one. Now we go on to something more complicated, with a one-versus-two sortie, one fighter against two targets, and moving on to two fighters against one target, so now you have to get a pair of fighters on to the target.

'Looking further down the variety of exercises, we send off the guy against a target that is flying lights-off at night. So there's no room for any cheating in that intercept as you just can't see him; so you'll have to get him on radar, cruise in and visually identify him. If you use the light from the moon and reflections from the sea you can sometimes make out the shape of an aircraft. And however hard you might try to concentrate on the radar information, you can look out and just catch a glimpse and know he's out there in the right place; but that only applies to the pilot, as the navigator can't see what's out in front anyway. However, once all these sorties are successfully completed, you're then allocated on the board as being Limited Combat Ready, and next time the Q programme comes out you're off on QRA, Quick Reaction Alert. That's something we really push for, to get the ready to hold QRA. We're doing a QRA period at the moment, and it's taking four crews off the squadron every day, to fulfil that commitment. At Wattisham we look after Southern QRA, which we share on rotation with Coningsby; and on the station here, it's shared out between us on 74 Squadron and 56, the other Phantom unit based here. So we end up holding QRA for about two to three months out of every year. Southern QRA has never really attracted much activity, as most of the incursions into our airspace take place so far away to the North. But for example we did launch Q-One yesterday, which was in the air for about six hours.'

On to the next phase, Low Level phase two: 'They start off two-versus-one and two-versus-two, then low level PIs, Practice Intercepts, one-against-one then two-against-one, and then two-versus-many. On a day like today, for example, you could go up as a pair, sit on a CAP, a Combat Air Patrol pattern, and pinpoint lots of targets out there. Then the second phase of the combat, when we get into the turning and burning business, the old Battle of Britain type of stuff. Normally the pilots will start off with a base height of eight thousand feet, and when you're combat ready, with the Boss's blessing, you can go down to five thousand feet; and you fly either radar to visual — where you go out to about forty miles using a radar station such as Neatishead and work out an entry into the fight — or you do it visually, where you just turn out and then turn back inbound. It's a very good pilot-handling exercise, teaching you to use the aircraft, although these days maybe it's a bit debatable whether it's a useful kind of exercise in reality, because so many aircraft can turn better than the Phantom. Some would say that, okay, if you're going to die, you might as well do it after a good fight rather than just running away, but obviously they have to learn the combat skills, how to handle the Phantom properly in a close-in fight. That's the ACT phase two, and that is sometimes engineered to coincide with the times when we go out to Decimomannu, where they have the Air Combat manoeuvring Instrumentation range, and we can do all this out there, where we can fly with different types of aircraft. If you're flying two-versus-two with Phantoms, you can have a problem. Are you the good guy or the bad guy? You can't really tell the difference. Out at Deci you can have Hornets, Mirage F1s, German Phantoms, loads of different types out there.

'Then you have the Combat Ready phase work-up. What we're preparing for is when we go off on exercise, the guys will be a combat-ready crew, and they can do everything that can be thrown at them. So you've got things like day scrambles and night scrambles, a combat-ready check, which is normally a guy leading a four-ship against a pre-arranged number of aircraft from another station. Sometimes we would use fifty-six here at Wattisham and we'll set up a Combat Air Patrol over Blakeney, Penrith, or over Wales, and they'll lead the four-ship in. They'll brief it and sometimes you wouldn't even know if you've got targets coming at you. You're just given a CAP position, a threat direction, and a possible type of threat, and it's up to you to brief it and fly it the best way you can. It can be done silently without any radio communication, just with light signals from the control tower for take-off, all sorts of things. After that, when you reach the end of this phase, we have the traditional squadron festivities, the drinking of some ice-cold beer, you get your badge, and you're finally a fully qualified member of the squadron.'

As a regular member of the front-line squadron, the fighter pilot is now able to lead a variety of missions: 'Officially, the pilot can now do anything that we can throw at him. However there are still different levels of experience, and obviously you're always learning until the day you finish flying. When you get to the bottom of this long list of work-up exercises, you've still got loads to learn, but you're allowed to do everything by then; and you'll be put into positions where, for example, a guy might be given a four-ship to lead, with a qualified four-ship leader in the formation to keep an eye on him, and then get his four-ship check out of the way so he's qualified for that. We've always got to have somebody in the tower, for example, to supervise the flying. So when they've done a certain amount of flying they'll get a tick in the box to say that they're able to supervise the flying. After about eighteen months he might be considered to sit on the desk here in the operations room. There's lots more he has to do even after he is combat ready. At this stage, he'll probably be flying on average maybe one sortie per day, although some days we might fly two or three, and some weeks he might only fly once or twice in a whole week. It depends on a range of factors. At the moment we're holding QRA and while that is the case, QRA is paramount, and takes a lot of aircraft off us, because we have two Phantoms parked nearby here, fully armed on ten minutes' readiness — and if for any reason one of these develops a fault, another of our aircraft will have to be taken over there to go on to QRA. When we launched a QRA aircraft yesterday, we had another aircraft standing by, fully serviceable with a full weapons load, just in case the one that was flying went unserviceable while it was flying. So QRA takes aircraft out of our normal operations and we tend to be a little short of aircraft while we're holding QRA.

'Aircraft go through phases. They tend to come out in sympathy with each other. You can have every day for a week where you start off in the morning with a full fleet of serviceable aircraft, and after the first wave you've got nothing. On other weeks you find you have only two aircraft serviceable in the morning, so you plan a pairs sortie. On the second wave of flying you have four, and on the third you have six, and by the time night flying starts you have more aircraft available than you can shake a stick at. It just depends on circumstances, and you can't predict how many aircraft you're going to have available for training at any given time, although in a wartime situation things would be very different. Some sorties are planned well in advance, and put into the programme at an early stage, so if we have the aircraft to meet the requirement we'll go ahead and do it.

'On the manning side of things, when we're holding QRA, if the guy is on QRA duty the next day is a stand-down after a twenty-four hour duty. So, looking at the list, on this day for example, we have only seven crews available, but fifteen sorties planned; so if we do every-thing we plan to do on that day, everyone will get two trips. When we're not doing QRA, we still have people down in the Falkland Islands, on leave, and various other things, and maybe we would have fifteen crews available; so if we do fifteen sorties, that's only one each. We also need one person on the Ops desk here, and another in the tower. A typical briefing will take place about an hour before take-off, and the debrief will last maybe an hour and a half after landing. So in some situations, such as we have on the list here, a crew can just debrief, get a cup of coffee, go into the brief for the next sortie, and off they go again. So on that day they would be in here about half past seven in the morning, and the next time they will have a chance to do anything will be about a quarter to four in the evening, and if they get three sorties in the day . . . well, that would really fill the day.

'With air-to-air refuelling, even with a clean-wing Phan-tom with no external stores, we can fly a good two-hour sortie, and with a centre-line fuel tank a two and a half hour sortie is quite common, so if they do two of those in a day it would take up their time easily. On this sortie, we have a four-ship scheduled, and whoever gets this one as leader will be able to do more or less what he wants, within the constraints of the rules we have to work with. He might take the four-ship overland, do some two-versus-two air combat; he could organise maybe four Phantoms against six Jaguars from Coltishall, or something like that. It will be up to him as sortie leader to get the most training value out of the flight, if there are no specific aims allocated to the mission. All sorties are briefed with an aim in mind. The only time you end up flying around aimlessly is if you plan to go as a pair, you do a stream take-off and, as you roll down the runway, your number two goes unserviceable, so you get airborne as a singleton. Then you might decide to do a practice diversion to Leuchars, or something like that, just to do something of value. We would be too heavy to land straightaway, so we have to use some of the fuel.

'The hardest thing about air-to-air combat is trying to anticipate what the other guy is going to do. You have to work out his energy level. The high yo-yos, the low yo-yos, lag pursuit rolls, all the well-known manoeuvres are all designed to do the same thing, to put your aircraft behind his. You've got to know what *he's* doing, to decide what *you're* going to do, and it does take a long time to get the hang of it all. It needs constant practice, and I'll admit we don't do combat as much as we'd like to. We do things called day tactics. Whereas in combat both aircraft are offensive and each one is trying to shoot the other one down, in day tactics we can fly down to two hundred and fifty feet, and one aircraft flies defensive while the other is offensive. The defensive pilot can manoeuvre fairly hard within certain parameters, in order to avoid being shot down; but he is not manoeuvring to get on to the other guy's tail, and you still have to use the basic ACM manoeuvres.

'The weapons systems we use all have things in favour of their use or vice-versa, depending on the circumstances. The Sparrow or Sky Flash is a semi-active missile, so you need to lock your radar on to the other aircraft in order to fire the missile. When you lock on to the other aircraft, his RWR, his Radar Warning Receiver, will alert him to the fact that you are there. With the Sidewinder we have a totally passive missile, and the target aircraft is giving off infra-red, so the missile picks this up, and you can fire off your Sidewinder, and he doesn't know it's coming unless he actually sees you. But with an infrared missile you can be defeated if the target aircraft deploys infra-red decoys, throwing out flares, or hiding in cloud, as that will act as a good insulator, or you could hide in the sun — whereas all these things wouldn't work against a Sky Flash. So it does depend upon the circumstances. The ranges between the missile systems are also very different. Whilst it would be preferable to launch off a missile and turn for home, you still have to illuminate the target with your radar while the missile is in flight. If you turn away, the missile wants to know who turned off the lights, and it will lose the target. You will always try to fire from the longest range possible and if both aircraft in a fight have the same type of semi-active missiles, clearly the one who fires his off first is the one who is going to live. If the other guy fires first you're automatically on the defensive and you're having to sort out avoidance of his missile, getting out of the area, and then trying to get back in again.

'Both the Tornado F3 and the Phantom are capable of doing exactly the same jobs, but with the Tornado F3s based to the North, we obviously wouldn't expect to go flying up there in a wartime situation; we would be down here in Suffolk. Before the Tornado came along, the Leuchars Phantom squadrons were doing long-range intercepts way up to the North. The Tornado has got basically the same missile as we have, and as their missiles are updated, so will ours be in turn, so that we're capable of doing the job.'

And what about political matters? Has glasnost changed the ways in which the RAF fighter pilot does his job? Has Operation Desert Storm changed the way in which RAF crews see their role? A fighter pilot explains: 'I don't think anything will change in real terms for a long time, as you've got to suck it and see. Okay, some changes have been made, the USAF aggressor training aircraft that we worked with have been pulled out, but whether that decision was because of East–West relations or financial considerations, I don't know. I think there will always be a Nato certainly, because there are other threats apart from the Warsaw Pact. I don't see much changing for maybe five years or more, personally speaking, but I'm not a politician, I'm a Phantom pilot. Even if the whole world was holding hands, kissing each other, each country would still need to have the ability to defend itself, in case one of the other nations suddenly pulled its hands away and wanted to start a fight. There's always got to be that ability to defend yourself, and I imagine that in the future our defence spending might be reduced, but that won't be for a long time, and the political developments are all very new. Mr Gorbachev might get assassinated, someone else take over, and everything suddenly go back to the way things used to be, who knows? There certainly hasn't been an outbreak of gloom and doom, that we no longer have a future. The only gloom might be that we won't have as many QRA intercepts to fly, with less intrusions into our airspace to take care of.'

Having completed what must be one of the most demanding training courses to be found in any profession, the fighter pilot is now qualified to handle a multi-million-pound killing machine. There is little time on the front-line squadron to consider the years of learning, but one newly qualified Phantom pilot allows himself to consider his new position within the United Kingdom's defence armoury: 'It's certainly a very satisfying feeling to have actually reached a front-line squadron. We have quite a hard time, and it's a very demanding job. I wanted this job very much. My enthusiasm really came from my father, but I always thought it would be great to be a pilot. I joined the Air Training Corps, and that really focused my attention on the RAF, although initially I think I would have been happy to fly almost anything, but your views change as you work through all the training. Over here, life is very different to the BFTS type of environment when you're flying Jet Provosts or Tucanos. There's still a lot of niff-naffs, chores which have to be undertaken to ensure the smooth running of the squadron, officer-training types of duty, and I'm sure they are all very character building as they say, but they're still a pain in the ass. Over here on the squadron, though, duties all have a purpose. Back at Cranwell I really had no idea what it was going to be like, and it was only when I reached Valley that I made contact with some of the front-line fast-jet pilots, and they tell you what it's all about. At the Tactical Weapons Unit you're out of the red-and-white trainers, you're using weapons, and your instructors are all front-line types, and when you get to an Operational Conversion Unit you do finally see what the fighter pilot's life is really going to be like.

'It takes such a long time to get through all the training I'm sure many people could easily get fed up, and lose the will to carry on, especially when people are being chopped from training all around you. I do think it's a pity that you can't see more of what life on an operational squadron will be like, when you're going through the training. I've become much more practical as the years have gone by, and I remember how starry-eyed I was when I first joined.

'It was incredibly hard work, but I made it, and this is a great job to be in . . . The best.'

9

SPIKING THE TARGET

The Royal Air Force undertakes a wide variety of tasks, and a qualified fast-jet pilot is not necessarily destined to become a fighter pilot. Apart from the defensive tasks undertaken by the Phantom and Tornado F3s (in company with Hawk support), the RAF also maintains a large number of offensive aircraft, such as the Tornado GR1, the Jaguar and the Harrier.

With the outbreak of hostilities in the Middle East in January 1991, the RAF began to operate some of these attack aircraft 'for real' over Iraq and occupied Kuwait. The press initially speculated that the Gulf operation, codenamed Desert Storm, would be a swift and decisive conflict, but the Pentagon and the British Ministry of Defence held a more realistic view from the outset. Crucial to their plans were the continual bombing sorties flown by RAF Tornado and Jaguar GR1s against the heavily defended Iraqi positions. These attacks were pressed home despite the danger, and in the knowledge that crews were being shot down.

To the outsider, however, one initially surprising development was the decision by the British to send Buccaneers to the Gulf, little more than a year before their scheduled retirement.

The reason for the 30-year-old Buccaneers being put into active service in their twilight years was the specialist weaponry they carried, and the equally specialised missions flown by their crews. Laser-guided bombs, which can be aimed precisely on targets with a laser beam, could be carried by both the Tornado and the Jaguar, but the Buccaneer crews specialised in 'laser designation' — illuminating targets with 'Pave Spike' pods.

In understanding the details of what Buccaneer flying is about, only so much can be gleaned by talking to the crews. The most effective way of learning is, as so often, simply to do it. Thanks to a huge amount of co-operation from the RAF, I was permitted to do just that, and to fly with a Buccaneer crew on a training mission, during which the aircraft could be demonstrated in its operational environment.

Situated on the shores of the Moray Firth, Lossiemouth, is a bleak landscape of grass, heather and concrete, littered with huge hangars (once used by the Fleet Air Arm) and HASs (Hardened Aircraft Shelters). It is one of the Royal Air Force's busiest airfields, providing a home for a wide variety of aircraft types, and a temporary base for an endless line of visitors destined for the nearby low flying areas, where the RAF is allowed to fly below the usual 250 feet height limit.

The two HAS complexes house the Buccaneers of Nos. 12 and 208 Squadrons, which form the basis of the RAF's anti-shipping strike force. The two units are assigned to SACLANT (Supreme Allied Commander Atlantic), operating exclusively in the maritime environment as part of No. 18 Group.

Like any other front-line squadron, 208 has a dedicated complex of briefing facilities, shelters, and support facilities, all 'hardened' against NBC (Nuclear, Biological and Chemical) attack, and the rather austere concrete 'village' is surrounded by a wall of barbed wire, guarded by the RAF Regiment during exercises (when wartime conditions are simulated). The various buildings are divided into the usual 'hard' and 'soft' areas (i.e. those which are strengthened to withstand attack, and those that are not), and the Buccaneer crews move freely to and from each area. Buried in this private citadel, Buccaneer operations are seldom seen by any 'outsider' . . .

The first task any Buccaneer 'back-seater' must perform, civilian or not, is to become familiar with his working environment. Lossiemouth has a Buccaneer simulator; an authentic representation of a real two-man cockpit, providing an ideal place for a civilian to get to know his temporary 'office' a little more intimately. There's no such thing as a free ride in a Buccaneer, as there are some important jobs (albeit very simple ones) that have to be done by the occupant of the navigator's position. The main responsibility is the control of the fuel supply. On the forward position of the left instrument console is a small control panel with five toggle switches and three corresponding dials. These control the fuel flow from the two underwing tanks (if fitted) and the bomb bay tank, as well as a further reserve housed inside the rotating bomb door itself. It is this last which gives the Buccaneer its distinctive bulging appearance. The fuel has to be fed into the aircraft system as required, and the gauges have to be constantly monitored. If the appropriate switch isn't thrown at the right time, the fuel lubrication system could overheat and catch fire.

Directly opposite the fuel supply controls, on the right forward console, are the controls for the IFF (Identification Friend/Foe) and SSR (Secondary Surveillance Radar) system. Most RAF and civilian airfields now utilise SSR, allowing radar controllers to keep a constant tally of aircraft callsigns, heights and flight paths, and it is the navigator's responsibility to control this function if required. On the main forward instrument panel are the drift variation switches for the pilot's bomb-aiming facility, with a set of weapons station selection switches on the side of the left-hand cockpit wall.

The crowded cockpit's most noticeable piece of furniture is the radar scope, wedged into the left-hand side of the instrument panel. Usually fitted with a tubular shade, the mode, brightness and contrast controls for the display are placed immediately to its right. The main radar controls (including the 'off', 'standby' and 'active' selections) are over on the right console. There are one or two other items of interest too, such as the VHF/UHF radio, the altimeter, compass, speed indicator, and radar altimeter, just visible on the pilot's instrument panel.

It takes a couple of hours to become fully confident in knowing just what piece of equipment is placed where, by which time the initially rather forbidding 'black hole' looks a little more friendly.

The need to dress appropriately means a visit to the flying clothing section, where suitable kit is issued and coaxed on — sometimes with considerable effort. First come the longjohns, huge woollen socks and a roll-neck sweater, over which the familiar flying overalls are worn. The weighty boots rarely, if ever, fit without a struggle. Over one's legs and stomach go the anti-g trousers (referred to as the 'g-suit'), and with the aid of clips and long zip fasteners, this inflatable structure is pushed and pulled into place, before being tightened to individual size by means of various adjustment laces. The aircrew helmet is the next delight in store, and with a struggle the assisting NCO adjusts a suitably sized item to sit 'comfortably' on one's head. The fit is tight, and it has to be so, as the fast-jet environment (high-g conditions) would soon shift a loose-fitting helmet, and the impact of an ejection would render a badly fitted helmet positively dangerous. The oxygen mask is then attached, and this too has to make a tight fit, not only to ensure a good supply of air/oxygen, but to safeguard against any poisonous fumes which might invade a cockpit. The mask also forms part of an overall facial guard against birdstrikes (which can smash a canopy, and blind aircrew if not protected). As more and more aircraft are fitted with

MDC (Miniature Detonating Cord) systems, the possibility of an accidental canopy shatter is also increasingly present. After checking that the RT lead and microphone (fitted into the mask) are functioning, and that the head set fitted into the helmet is also performing loud and clear, the clothing can be stored away until it is time to fly.

As well as making these mental and physical preparations to fly in a Buccaneer, passengers in such aircraft are required by the RAF to be certified as 'fit' by their own medical officers. You don't have to be Superman to qualify, but equally the RAF does like to be fairly confident that a passenger is going to survive the experience in one piece, and great care is also taken to establish whether the occupant will be sufficiently small to fit into the confines of the rear cockpit. (Fortunately my six-foot-two height could be accommodated.)

The next day starts early, and a MT section minibus calls at the station entrance to carry personnel to the 208 Squadron complex, a five-minute drive away, around the airfield perimeter. The first call is to the crew room, where the duty pilots and navigators are sampling the endless supply of coffee, tea and biscuits. The wall-mounted television is tuned into the BBC's 'Breakfast Time' programme, and the assembled officers divide their attention between their refreshments, the TV news, and various magazines, newspapers and station information sheets. The scene is a comfortable one, and there are few uniforms here, other than the traditional flying overalls. An occasional visitor walks by carrying a helmet ('bonedome' is the accepted phrase), life jacket, and anti-g trousers. His journey will lead him just a few yards from the crew room to a locked door which will require the insertion of a code number to allow entrance. Immediately next to this door is another, larger version — an enormous steel monster with a huge locking wheel. Moving this door requires considerable effort, so it is generally left open during normal peacetime conditions.

The floor inside this entrance is not solid. One walks along the corridor on a raised metal grille, a few inches

above a pit containing fuller's earth. Suddenly the surroundings take on a more serious appearance — we're in
an airlock. Following the one-way system, thoughtfully
signposted by arrows (wartime NBC contamination regulations dictate that the wearers of 'dirty' clothing follow
just one route into the building, and 'clean' personnel
another route out), one enters a second squadron crew
room, this time deserted, with a dormitory visible to one
side, and a kitchen and washroom opposite. Few people
have time for rest or refreshment here, as the next room
is the 'business end' of 208 Squadron's operations — the
Ops room, containing all current information on the
unit's operations. The wall carries a large visual display
which shows the status of each Buccaneer (weapons fit,
location, etc.), the schedule of missions for the day, crews
involved, times, fuel states, and much more. To the left
side is a large diagram of the HAS complex. In the centre
of the room a SNCO engineering controller sits at a long
console, in company with an Ops control SNCO and a
senior squadron executive officer. They are effectively
running the day's operations, in direct connection with all
sections of the squadron, and the outside world. During
exercises the 'War Exec' would sit here and co-ordinate
208's operations.

Through an internal window, the Buccaneer crews can
be seen, hard at work in the Planning Room — a larger
area containing two spacious tables, map stowage shel-
ves, and wall-mounted information connected with day-
to-day flight planning. The room is invariably littered
with maps of all descriptions, as the pilots and navigators
deliberate over high- and low-level routes, drawing up
mission maps with the aid of pens, rulers, protractors,
compasses and pocket calculators. The adjacent door
leads to the briefing room, where the pre-flight briefing
for the next sortie is ready to begin. It's going to be a two-
ship exercise, intended to include almost every aspect
of Buccaneer operations. The four men involved in the
operation, including myself and the Commanding Officer
of the Squadron, referred to as 'The Boss', prepare to
digest the appropriate details from the formation's

appointed leader, who stands at the front of the group, beside an overhead projector.

'Okay, good morning, gentlemen. The aim of today's sortie is to go off and use some weaponry and do some low level nav, with a main aim of doing Buccaneer-to-Buccaneer AAR. We also have a VC10 as a bonus, but everything is aimed at getting the Buccaneer tanker. So write down the details please, and look up when you're ready.' The crew glance up at the projector's wall display and scribble the important points on to their knee pads, fitted into their flying overalls. The morning's weather details have already been covered, leaving the officer to explain the mission plan: 'Okay, I'll carry on now . . . Crews, myself and Mike leading, with the Boss and Tim flying number two. Call-sign Skull One and Two, and the HASs . . . we've got one-six-eight in twenty-four, and you've got two-eight-seven in twenty-two. We have the SX and you have the CE. Your load is two inerts, probably on station three, and two flash on station four . . . drop the inerts, please. We have the standard stuff . . . three KG's. Eighteen-K fuel for ourselves, and nineteen for you, Boss.' From this barrage of abbreviations the crew learn that the sortie is to include the use of some underwing stores (in this case two inert bombs), some low-level navigation over land, and some AAR (Air-to-Air Refuelling), using both a VC10 and another Buccaneer, equipped with a 'buddy' refuelling pod. The call sign for the formation is 'Skull', and the aircraft are housed in Hardened Aircraft Shelters (nos. 24 and 22). The fuel loads are 18,000 and 19,000 lbs. respectively, and the underwing stores are fixed in 'SX' and 'CE' configurations (code letters for two specific combinations).

The brief continues: 'Weather here is quite nice, looking out the door. Steve will go out to help you and set up all the switches, Tim, so there should be very little for you to do, other than fuel management and looking after yourself, okay? Then you can start up and do the checks as you require, Boss, just to be there for the check-in. We'll taxi out to whatever runway is in use, one-zero at the moment, and we'll line up as per the wind . . . twenty second stream . . . I'll be going blown, then you chase after me to catch up. Join at whatever formation you require, and if you need any photos, Tim, just tell the Boss what you want. I'll try and go for Arrow, but if you want to come in close, please make sure I know so that I don't rack on the bank. However, whatever you like. Arrow or Battle. En route to Rosehearty . . . formation I've already covered, whatever you require, Tim, for your business, just put in your request to the Boss, and he'll clear it through me, so I don't go and do anything silly and bash into him! When we've completed the sortie, we'll come back in here for a pairs approach. On one-zero an SRA, and hopefully on two-eight a PAR or we may just do it visually, whatever we feel like at the time. Just make sure you're upwind of us, Boss, and we'll do hand signals. We'll overshoot the pairs approach at four hundred feet, I'll put the airbrake in, and there'll be a pause. When the airbrake's fully travelled I'll gently start to bring the power up, so the airbrake's your signal for when I'm about to start overshooting. We'll try to keep it nice and tight. Whoever is towards the downwind leg will turn downwind away from the other guy, a positive turn, and get themselves in the circuit. Landing separation is twenty seconds minimum, and remember other people's circuits as well, so you won't get cleared to land inside that anyway. All through the exercise, if we go u/s you'll have to wait until we get ourselves another aeroplane, and if you go u/s, we'll wait for you.'

The phrase 'going blown' refers to the Buccaneer's BLC (Boundary Layer Control) system, which blows high pressure air (bled from the engines) over the control surfaces, thus creating greater lift, and allowing the aircraft to fly at slower speeds. Normal Lossiemouth departures are performed 'un-blown', but for this sortie the main (8,393 feet) runway is temporarily closed, and the shorter (6,023 feet) secondary runway will be used instead. SRA (Surveillance Radar Approach) and PAR (Precision Approach Radar) are different types of ground controller-guided approach patterns.

The navigator now continues the briefing: 'Time

check . . . we've had royal flights and there's one to the south so it shouldn't affect the sortie, but we've had to sign for it. Danger areas . . . there are two that affect the sortie, eight-oh-nine south which is active to eight thousand feet, so we'll transit above that on our way out to the north, and six-oh-nine, plus these over here which are suppressed throughout Priory, so we need to keep out of them. Were we for some reason needing to work to the south here, we would certainly need to keep out of six-oh-nine, six-oh-seven and six-oh-eight for Priory. Safety altitude, we can use five-point-five throughout for this part of the high ground, and remember there are lumps of rock sticking out of the ground around there. Notams . . . there are none that affect us, although there is a late warning that I'll point out when we outbrief, of a crop sprayer. Airways: again we'll be transmitting over the advisory routes, but we'll be getting a radar service from Scottish. If our internal chatter is too much I'll ask for a frequency they don't mind us blathering about on. Coming back low level we should be under all those. Pressures we'll take when we walk. Fuel is one at ten, and probably the same after the tanking, or Bingo, minus whatever it is after the tanking, so that we know after all the different tanking events going on, where we start from. Bingo two of five-point-five is a fuel from about the Orkneys, to come back low level through the Pentland Firth, a fairly straight recovery on five-point-five. Okay, the plan then . . . if it's two-eight, a big right turn, or if it's one-zero, straight ahead, more or less heading zero-nine-zero out towards Rosehearty. It's five minutes from abeam the lighthouse, so we'll be in at the target at four-twenty knots. We'll go in Battle with you on the left, and when we're abeam we'll turn downwind and increase to five hundred knots and squawk four-three-two-zero. There are helicopters around there, Tim, so keep your eyes open as well, and if you see anything, talk about it and tell us. Okay, we're in there for two passes, probably visual laydown, and we'll RV at Troup Head, off the second pass, although you'll probably be fairly close behind us I'd guess, and you call us to turn, jink or whatever, right? We'll then set off round this little low level nav . . . We'll try and fly this route, and you feel free to move around us as you see fit for a good line for your photos, Tim. The only thing to beware of on this route is Balmoral out here to the right.

'That'll take us to Montrose and we go under this airway here as well, so if there's weather down here, the base area level is six-five. And that'll take us to Montrose . . . measure the heading . . . looks like zero-eight-zero from Montrose, climbing up to two-three-zero initially, and we'll go across to Scottish then, two-four-eight-four. We'll call when clear. To RV with the tanker, call-sign India India eight-five. We'll climb out heading up into the towline talking to Scottish, and then hand over to Buchan. Then we'll endeavour to do the VC10 tanking. You can take pictures, we can manoeuvre, or do what we like . . . they're very flexible, the VC10s, and they'll probably do what we ask for. We'll wait with them, hopefully until the Buccaneer tanker turns up, callsign India Echo Uniform three-three, from his Tornado task, okay? He'll try and get there between fifteen hundred and fifteen-thirty, so he should join us on the towline, and he'll probably take a bit of fuel as well, so we can both watch that, and then we'll set off, heading up towards Duncansby Head, to do our Buccaneer–Buccaneer tanking. So we'll leave Buchan, go back to Scottish, try and get a quiet frequency, and do our Buccaneer–Buccaneer tanking on that leg. The tanker will go home and we will let down to low level, heading about north from around the Pentland Firth, to look at a tactic . . . and we'll do half a Delta; Simon will brief it. Then we'll follow round the Orkneys and if we've got the fuel and time, we can wander around there as much as you like. There are light aircraft around the Orkneys, so keep a lookout for those. And then back through the Pentland Firth, past the oil rigs back to Lossiemouth, okay? We'll commence recovery on the Bingo two call . . . Any questions?'

The fuel calls are again mentioned, chiefly because things are far from straightforward when aerial refuelling is included. The pre-briefed fuel figures obviously have to be updated, depending on the amount of fuel taken by each receiver. The phrase 'squawk' refers to the IFF/SSR system, describing the act of transmitting an information pulse to the ground receiver. 'Buchan' and 'Scottish' are area radar controlling authorities. 'Priory' is the name of a three-day RAF exercise, taking place at various RAF fighter stations, involving the use of a variety of reserved airspace.

The pilot now takes over the briefing again: 'First task then, we go to Rosehearty and drop our bombs. Now, you've already been shown the bomb distributor, I believe, Tim, okay? There aren't many switches you need be too worried about on there, apart from the Start, Stop and the Singles switch, and we'll cover those fully at the end of the briefing. Rosehearty range then . . . we'll do two passes with the twenty-eight inerts, and the three-kgs for us. Rosehearty range is the call sign and stud seventeen. Target two, which is a raft — as you'll see it's a small orange raft — sits out there in the middle of the water. Sometimes you can see it and sometimes you can't. Sea level and danger area SOP, and what we're really looking for there is to put the bomb close to the target, so you don't bomb any fishing boats, and the bomb ought to drop between a thousand foot over and a thousand foot short. The Boss will make sure he's quite happy that the bomb's not going to hit anything else, and then he'll call singles; that is your cue, Tim, to make the final safety switch selection from Off, and it should already be Start-three and Stop-three, okay? That's providing the inerts are on three, which they ought to be, but you'll check that in the book when you get out there, Boss, two-five-one is the heading that we aim to drop the bombs on, and what they give you the score off. We'll go for a visual split, and make sure you're a good twenty seconds behind, and we'll RV at five nautical miles north off Troup Head . . . and as soon as you're aboard call us, and we'll head off on our route. The wind we've got . . . we're looking at a slight southerly drift of fifteen knots, but really at the bombing height it's plus ten, and your own speed is five hundred and four knots, and we'll work our own out. Now Tim, you want five-point-one set to allow for the weight and the type of attack you're doing, and the correction of the aircraft. Forget about wind velocity, the Boss will offset for that . . . if you lay forty feet into the wind for every ten knots of wind, a quick look at the wind, and just aim offside. The raft is thirty foot long as a gauge itself. We're looking for the bombs inside one-forty feet. Once you're complete on the range you must make the switches safe, Tim, and we'll make a switches safe call to remind everyone to do it, so remember you're setting Start-eight and Stop-one, and the mode switch goes to Off, and the Boss will make his safe.'

The 'Singles', 'Stop', and 'Start' references are connected with the weapons station selection and release switches, which are controlled from the rear cockpit, although the actual firing signal is made by the pilot.

'Okay, the low nav bit. We'll run along there and all sit on track, but if you want to do anything, Tim, like taking photos, just say, otherwise sit back with the Boss and he'll give us some cross cover. If we do hit bad weather at this stage, remember that there are solid centres in those clouds, so get away in an emergency and abort from low level. You know how to squawk emergency, Tim? If we end up going into the airway we will tell you, but obviously we'll try not to do it. Happy with that? All right, we'll coast up, then go up to the tanker. First of all then, it's India India eight-five, a VC10 at fifteen hundred to fifteen thirty on the two line. Buchan will get a frequency for them, and expect us to take Tacan five-eight to get a range from him. He's planning to be flight level two-five-zero, and we'll join with an RV Charlie using full RT. If you spot the tanker before us, Boss, then try and get our eyes on to it, and we'll get ourselves aboard nice and swiftly . . . if we need the airbrake I'll take it, I won't call it. We'll join on the port in Arrow initially, and we'll refuel in the order one and two, and we'll take two-K apiece. Have you been to a VC10 before, Boss? Well, if we've got a half-hour slot it might be worth taking a few dry prods as well, but if our tanker has called up we'll just take two-K and get him in and fuelledup. We'll depart with our tanker to Duncansby. We'll call the VC10 and when we speak to him with our requirements, we'll tell him that we have a press photographer in the back of number two. While we're in that state we will hopefully have been joined by India Echo Uniform three-three, and he will come in and tank. We will have gone through first, and we'll initially sit off to starboard and wait for him to finish. When he's complete and dropping out, we'll start to move out into tight Battle formation so that he can move up on the inside. We'll have passed on our requirements on leaving, so we'll turn off there. And then it's back to Scoots . . . hopefully not in that fashion there . . . ' (the magnetic Buccaneer shape being used to illustrate the positions suddenly performs its own dramatic dive from the blackboard, amid hoots of laughter).

'So, on to Duncansby, flight level as required, probably around the two-fifty mark. Once clear we'll try to do it as silently as we can, so as not to clutter up the Scottish frequency, but if you want any inputs, Tim, speak up and tell the Boss what you want and he'll tell us. We'll tank in the order one and two, initially for one-K, but if you want us to take dry prods and stuff, we'll change headings to get the sun out of the way, just tell us, as at that stage we'll have plenty of gas. Once we're complete we'll be on the starboard and we'll clear to low-level. Emergencies at any stage during the tanking are SOP the diversions, and you can go to Leuchars, otherwise back to Lossie. If you have a problem we will come with you and drop you off somewhere, but if we're with the Buccaneer tanker, we'll let him take you home, and if we've got a problem we'll go into Leuchars. The VC10, in case you can't remember, Boss, has quite a lot of dihedral which is quite disorientating, if there's a bit of cloud around, but otherwise it's quite smooth, and it's a nice big basket which tends to wobble a bit . . . they're very good. Missed approach then is as standard, obviously you've probably got something wrong, so return to your stabilised position, check trim and have another go. If there's any damage to your aircraft, then it's into Leuchars, and we'll come with you. Right, any points on refuelling? . . . It's the main reason for going up there anyway . . . Now the tactic . . . to make it nice and simple we'll do a Delta-two experimental, one and two in the fifteen hundred yards swept position. We'll use two hundred feet to get it away from the sea, and please watch the weather there. Then climb out . . . if the weather's funny, then try and get yourself into close formation and ease away from the water, and if not we'll just pull up, call our heading, and you take us through. Escape manoeuvre as SOP, and use instruments in the toss recovery. Once you're happily back on the horizon get me visual and follow me out. Switches, well if you like you could do a vari-toss but you won't have the offsets . . . follow me up using four g.

'To let you have an idea what we're talking about, Tim, we're simulating attacking a ship which is probably undefended, and we're dashing in to toss a bomb at it from about three and a half nautical miles, okay? So what we do is at thirty miles we go up to five-fifty knots to get there nice and quickly as we come over the horizon, and at fifteen miles we'll call "Bananas"; a ridiculous thing to say, but what it means is that the target is at fifteen miles on the nose. We'll dash in, and at three and a half miles we'll pull up. You will hear us say "Standby . . . now" and then you'll hear "beep" which is us going up, and five seconds later the Boss will have started his stopwatch and will follow us. After four seconds the bombs would come off, heading towards the target, and the spikers, the guys down at the back, would begin spiking as you saw in the films earlier. We'll recover back the other way using four g, and providing you're visual, Boss, just call us and we'll begin doing our next business.'

The word 'spiker' is central to the world of Buccaneer operations. Inside the briefing room the Buccaneer crews are delighted to show video films of the aircraft in action, using the Paveway LGB (Laser-Guided Bomb) attack system. A 'spiker' is a suitably configured Buccaneer, carrying a Pave Spike laser designation pod on the port inner hardpoint. Once a target is identified, the pod is used to illuminate the aiming point for the LGBs, carried by accompanying Buccaneers or Tornado GR1s. The bombs are thrown into a huge parabolic trajectory in a 'toss' manoeuvre, and once the bombs have reached the upper limit of their flight path, the laser pod is brought into action, 'lasing' or 'spiking' the target. The bombs then lock on to the illuminated target, and fall with astonishing accuracy. A film shows a tiny wooden 'splash' target being obliterated by a concrete-filled inert LGB: 'We had this little raft with a couple of bed sheets tied to it . . . we split it into two parts with an inert LGB . . . it's a very reliable system.'

The briefing is nearing its conclusion: 'Right, fuel management: Tim, that's your main job on this sortie. The switches have all been explained, but when we're on the tanker you must switch the overloads off. Your bomb bay will probably be empty so switch the bomb door off . . . and also you can use the radar at any stage during the sortie, but put it on standby while we're tanking, so that you don't irradiate the poor guys. And pins . . . Steve will be with you when you strap in, to make sure they're all out, but when you come back in, before you unstrap, make sure you've got them all back in. There's no rush to get out unless it's on fire, in which case, run like hell! Generally then, Tim, on cockpit management, you've got plenty of kit with you so be careful where you put it, but at all times, if you're moving things around, make sure you can get to the ejection handle. If the Boss takes a bird in the face at low-level, and can't speak to you, you've got to be able to get out of there fairly quickly, otherwise he's briefed you on what's going to happen if you need to get out. Disorientation, now: if you feel funny and you don't know which way up you are, tell the Boss, and he'll tell you what's going on . . . hopefully. All right, for a low-level abort in emergency, get away from the ground. Right, now everything on this sortie should string together, however it doesn't take long for things to start going wrong, or for people to start cancelling, so we'll stay flexible and we'll talk about what we need on the radio. Any points to add, Mike? Boss? Tim? . . . '

The briefing is completed, and while the crews leave the darkened room, and gather at a small window looking into the Ops room, where the last-minute detail changes or confirmations are made (known as 'out-briefing,), I go to gather my remaining items of equipment. The life-saving jacket is a particularly cumbersome piece of kit, but it serves the wearer well, and is standard to almost every RAF operation, often even those that do not include flights over water (there are plenty of lakes around). Inside the 'Mae West' (a name still applied to this day) is a radio homing beacon, which automatically transmits after ejection for the benefit of rescue helicopters. Also included is a set of mini flares, again designed to attract the attention of one's rescuers. Attached just below one's knees are the leg restraint garters, suitably adjusted so that a pair of buckles stand proud, to accept a pair of lanyards connected to the ejection seat. When the seat is fired the lanyards retract into the seat base, snatching in both legs to prevent them from flailing about, smashing against the cockpit walls, and being broken. Finally, a pair of white kid leather gloves complete the attire — not only are the gloves comfortably thin (to allow the effective operation of the aircraft switches), but they are fireproof too.

The nearby Hardened Aircraft Shelters are arranged in a distinctly untidy fashion; there are no neat rows here, but instead an arrangement cunningly designed to thwart a marauding bomber's attempt to destroy more than one HAS on one bombing run. Inside HAS 22, its doors already open, is Buccaneer S2B XT 287, waiting with an accompanying ground crew. Two Buccaneers are regularly housed in a single HAS, although in wartime conditions only one aircraft 'lives' in each HAS, sealed off against the unpredictable external conditions.

Inside the shelter, the Buccaneer appears quite huge. It's not a small aircraft by any standards, and the bulge of the belly tank and the oddly shaped 'area-ruled' fuselage give the aircraft an impression of great size and weight. Climbing into the cockpit, laden with flying clothing, helmet and camera, is itself something of a feat. Some careful footwork allows the back-seater to step over the side of the fuselage and stand on the seat, before slotting his feet on to the floor and sitting back, whilst holding on to the instrument panel coaming. Once settled as comfortably as possible (ejection seats are not known for their softness), the first task is to connect the PEC (Personal Equipment Connector) to the socket on the right-hand side of the seat. This rubber-tubed attachment supplies oxygen to the mask and high pressure air to the g-suit. On the other side of the seat is the PSP (Personal Survival Pack) clip, which attaches the wearer to the dinghy pack (slotted into the seat pan). Also fixed to the seat is a small window containing a weight figure dial which is adjusted to match the seat occupant's all-up weight, in order to give the seat the correct ejection trajectory.

Next come the leg restraints, the two blue cords threaded in turn through the twin leg buckles, before their plugged ends are inserted into a pair of sockets at the base of the seat. They have to be attached now as it's particularly difficult to secure them when fully strapped in. The straps are pulled up from between the legs and from over the shoulders, all routed and attached to a quick-release box positioned over the crotch. Once each strap is successfully connected, the complete harness is tightened (each strap in turn), until it is almost impossible to move one's body. For most flight conditions, even during quite severe manoeuvring, the straps don't need to be painfully tight, but the wearer can be certain that his flight will not end with an ejection. If it does, even an inch or so of slack can (and sometimes does) result in broken bones; the seat's rapid progress from the cockpit makes no concession to the fragile occupant.

Finally, the bonedome: this too is pushed and pulled into place, and the oxygen mask is clipped into position. The clear visor is slid down, and the back-seater is ready to fly, already hot and sticky inside the dark shelter. The combined smell of oil, fuel and rubber mask does nothing to improve the conditions. (In wartime, this whole procedure might have to be conducted in seconds, with the added inconvenience of an NBC mask.)

The Boss arrives in the HAS, and after consulting the ground crew, he takes a walk around the airframe, searching for tell-tale signs of danger. The ground engineers have already thoroughly inspected every inch of the aircraft, but nobody gives up the chance of a last-minute glance, just in case. He then climbs into the cockpit and begins his pre-start checks, his actions visible from the back seat, thanks to the slightly off-centre seating arrangement. The rear seat is positioned just to the right of the centre line, the pilot's to the left, allowing an over-the-shoulder view of activity in the front 'office'. The ground crew wind the Palouste air starter into action, and the HAS suddenly fills with noise, muffled only by one's helmet (the ground crew wear ear defenders and work either by RT connection or hand signals). The two Spey turbofans rumble into life and the noise becomes even more overpowering, blasts of hot kerosene vapour rolling around inside the shelter. The ground crew monitor the operation of the flying controls, signalling (by hand) to the pilot that each moveable surface is operating correctly. The seat pins are removed from each seat, and stowed in their flight positions. The sound of our 'playmate' (callsign 'Skull One') crackles into the RT; they too are ready to taxi and with a blast of power from the engines the huge monster lurches forward, making a brief curtsey, to check the brake function. As the Buccaneer rolls out into the daylight the canopy is slid shut and locked, and the environment suddenly becomes rather more user-friendly.

Skull One rumbles past our nose, heading for the runway, and Skull Two carefully tucks in behind, on to the weaving taxiway, HASs to either side. In the relative calm, the RT chatter switches between the two aircraft and the control tower, to a persistent background of regular hisses. The crew's microphones tend to amplify the sound of breathing, which itself requires some adjustment, in order to come to terms with the uncomfortable oxygen mask and the 'on-demand' oxygen system. The two 'doll's-eyes' indicators attached to the left console wink from black to white, in time with one's inhalation — it's reassuring to see that both occupants of this aircraft are at least breathing! The control tower gives the two pilots air traffic clearance to take off, with a last-minute update on the wind speed and direction, and the Buccaneers roll on to the white-painted 'keyboard' markings at the threshold of Lossiemouth's runway 10, where a row of sparkling lights runs down each side of the concrete to the horizon.

A last check that everything is in order, and the first Buccaneer, on the left-hand side of the runway, edges forward, accompanied by a cloud of dirty, brown-coloured smoke. The engine blast gently buffets against our fuselage as our own engines wind up to full power. The Buccaneer is ready to go, held on the brakes, everything shaking . . . twenty seconds on the stopwatch, and the brakes are released. Ahead of us, the first Buccaneer is visible, just above the horizon, trailing a brown exhaust plume. We are rushing down the runway with steady acceleration (no 'neck-breaking' reheat in the Buccaneer) and the 1000-foot markers roll by with increasing rapidity. The end of the runway is clearly visible and getting closer as the wheels gently ease from the concrete and tuck smartly into their raised positions, with what seems to be just a few feet of runway to spare (take-off from Lossie's short runway can never be described as mundane!).

Once comfortably clear of the ground, we turn left towards the coastline, skirting the small town of Lossiemouth, which sweeps by beneath our port wingtip. The airspeed is already up to the briefed 420 knots as the trees give way to sea, the weapons range a few miles distant. The Buccaneer has an enviable reputation for ultra-smooth low-level flight, and the first few minutes in the back seat confirm that the ride really is exceptionally comfortable. The first-time occupant automatically expects the usual fast-jet 'rough-ride', and the first impressions of the Buccaneer's conditions are surprising, to say the least.

XV168 (Skull One) has already assumed a loose battle formation, and can just be seen down on the horizon, a couple of miles to our left. Rosehearty weapons range has already cleared both aircraft into its area, and the speed begins to rise as the aircraft gently descend to 200 feet. With the needle indicating 500 knots, the Boss turns the aircraft through 180 degrees towards the raft target, as XV168 dashes in ahead of us. The weapons release switches are selected, and the Boss calls to me to throw the final switch to make the small practice bomb 'live'. As the target approaches, the Boss calls out a verbal countdown, pressing the release button on his control column as the brightly painted raft rushes past beneath our fuselage. Round the range circuit for a second pass, and the two attacks are complete, the weapons switches placed back to their safe positions, as the coastline rapidly approaches. Pulling up to overfly the small coastal towns, the two aircraft slowly edge together to form a tighter formation for the overland navigational exercise, descending once more when clear of the main areas of population.

Back to 250 feet on a heading of 225 degrees, the duo race towards the first turning point at Huntly, north-west of Aberdeen. The navigator's 1:500,000 map clearly shows the intended route, with one-minute intervals marked on a long, black line. Providing the pilot stays on course and maintains the speed at 420 knots, this Navex should be relatively easy. Sure enough, the small town comes into view on the three-minute mark, as predicted, and the next turn on to 196 degrees is initiated. The bleak Scottish landscape now becomes even more forbidding, and the weather is starting to close in. Balmoral should be somewhere to the right, but nobody seriously expects to see it; the royal residence is protected by a box of restricted airspace, and an intrusion into the area would be by accident rather than design. The rolling landscape gives a much greater impression of speed, and even this 'easy-rider' doesn't offer much comfort at low level over land. The two aircraft have settled into the usual bumpy race over the hillsides, passing all manner of sights, from tall pine trees to scattered sheep. Our route is designed to avoid overflying populated areas, but even so, the Boss keeps an eye open for any obvious places which can be avoided, and never stops keeping a lookout for bird concentrations. The weather is still deteriorating, and a darkened grey patch looms straight ahead, which threatens to throw the formation off its intended track. The clouds do sometimes have 'solid centres' (hillsides) and the leader elects to fly around the weather, promptly pulling sharply away to the left, streaming two condensation trails from the wingtips. XV168 flips smartly over, belly-up, and drops down into a valley, under the weather, as we turn back to the right, my g-suit increasing its vice-like grip as the rate of turn increases. Round the weather in a matter of seconds, the Boss quickly identifies Skull One again, and the formation is re-formed.

The next turn is on to 080 degrees, and the lead aircraft is now 200 to 300 yards ahead of XT287, as both aircraft roll on to their sides and sweep over the top of a bleak hillside. The wingtip condensation trails are accompanied by occasional sharp bursts of thick white cloud, which occasionally form around each aircraft. The weather really is bad, but the overall visibility is still acceptable, and both Montrose and the Scottish coastline come into view, the slow climb out of the low-level Navex beginning just half an hour after leaving Lossie. It's been an action-packed 30 minutes.

The ascent from the coast takes ten minutes, putting us into a refuelling area (a box of airspace reserved for air-to-air refuelling), roughly 30 miles east of Montrose. Our lead is in contact with the VC10 tanker which is already waiting inside the 'box', gently flying a wide racetrack circuit. The Boss spots the distant tanker, and moves us into position, formating on the VC10's port wing at 25,000 feet. We're in the land of perpetual sunshine above the clouds and the massive fin and the tailplane of the four-engined tanker sweeps majestically over the cockpits of XV168, as the Buccaneer edges in to take a careful stab at the starboard wing refuelling basket. We are invited to take up position behind the port basket, and we gently edge towards the rear of the tanker, before moving slowly forwards to the trailing basket. With a reassuring 'clunk' our probe makes a firm connection with the fuel vent, inside the basket. Fuel is flowing and we take on 2000 lbs of kerosene, high over the North sea. The Boss makes it look deceptively easy.

Buchan radar has directed a third Buccaneer into the refuelling box, this aircraft being configured as a tanker, carrying a hose drum unit (HDU) in a pod under the starboard wing. XV868 had already been hard at work further south, refuelling a formation of Tornados, and now it is the turn of the tanker pilot to take on some fuel for himself from the VC10. The Boss asks the VC10 captain (who is responsible for controlling the four-ship formation) if we can leave the standard refuelling formation, to adopt some rather more 'artistic' angles for the author's camera. As predicted, the VC10 crew are more than happy to oblige, so while the Buccaneer tanker replenishes its fuel supply, XV168 sits on the end of the second basket, performing a few 'dry' prods (linking up, but not taking any fuel) as practice. The Boss meanwhile takes XT287 into a whole variety of different positions, looking at the formation from each side, as well as from below and above.

Keeping a receiver plugged into a basket requires a great deal of concentration, especially over a long period, and for 'Skull One' this rendezvous must be something of a marathon: it is doubtless with some relief that the Buccaneer tanker completes its refuelling. The VC10 captain departs for the long flight back to Brize Norton, leaving the three Buccaneers to turn on to 314 degrees, descending back to low level.

Under control of Scottish radar, the next leg of the sortie takes the formation north-west towards the Orkneys, during which time a further refuelling rendezvous is made, this time between the two receiver aircraft and the Buccaneer tanker. XV868 trails the long hose and basket from the Mk. 20 refuelling pod, and 'Skull One' and 'Skull Two' each take 1000 lbs of fuel from the tanker, as the formation makes steady progress to the Orkneys, at 280 knots (the fuel hose's limiting speed is 290 knots).

Once complete, the tanker navigator reels in the basket, only to find that the last few feet of hose refuse to slide back into the pod. Some careful airspeed control results in the wing flaps being momentarily extended, which gives the hose a useful nudge, and the basket quickly pops back into the end of the pod. Descending slowly, the trio levels out at 250 feet, just off the north-east tip of the Scottish coast, sweeping past the famous John O'Groats scenery. The tanker pilot calls that he still has a little fuel in reserve, and offers to fly in formation with the basket extended once more, to allow the back-seater to gather a few more interesting pictures. The lowest refuelling height is 2000 feet, so no pilot could attempt actually to take on fuel at low level, but the Boss closes in on the port side of the tanker, as XV868 dashes along the coastline of the Orkneys, the basket waving in protest at the distinctly non-standard altitude.

After passing the famous 'Old Man of Hoy' landmark, the tanker sets course for Lossiemouth, while XV186 pulls into line abreast for a second pass along the coastline. The fulmars and gannets must have just settled on to their nests again after the first disturbance, as the two evil-looking monsters come hurtling round the cliff-tops again, leaving their wake of noise and smoke. Immediately to port is the stretch of water called Scapa Flow, a reminder of military conflicts of the past, and of the serious reality of the Buccaneer's business.

As if proof were needed of the Buccaneer's true capabilities, the final phase of this sortie starts over the Pentland Firth, just north of Lossie. The plan is to fly a 'Delta Two Experimental'; a suitable phrase to describe a two-ship simulated Paveway attack, that will represent the type of operations performed by Buccaneers during the Gulf War. Although today's demonstration won't include the release of any weapons, the manoeuvres will be exactly the same. If this was 'for real', additional Buccaneers or Tornado GRls would be trailing us at about 4000 to 5000 yards, carrying Pave Spike designation pods. The radar altitude reads 200 feet, and the speed has risen to 550 knots . . . we're really moving . . .

145

About forty miles from the target, the formation splits into two elements, with either two lead aircraft, or four if the formation is a six-ship. The two 'Spikers' carrying the laser designated pods always fly at the rear of the group. The aircraft are all widely separated, allowing each Buccaneer crew to maintain an effective lookout on the neighbouring aircraft's six-o'clock position, from where an attacking fighter is likely to make his attack. In this sort of formation it's quite possible to find an enemy fighter closing in on the tail of the lead aircraft, only to become 'sandwiched' in front of the Spiker, which will normally carry a Sidewinder missile. The Sidewinder is a very effective piece of self-defence equipment, although another very useful tactic is to 'drop one's knickers'; this graphic phrase describes the release of a 1000 lb retarded bomb in front of an attacking fighter, a measure almost as effective as a Sidewinder from the rear: 'Dropping a thousand-pounder in his face should certainly put him off his aim.' About twenty-five miles from the target, one of the aircraft will quickly pull up to locate and nominate a suitable target feature, giving the bearing and distance to the rest of the formation, before dropping back to wave-top height. In peacetime the attacks are usually flown down to 200 feet, although sometimes as low as 100 feet. The wartime limit, however, is only limited by the pilot's confidence and nerve, 50 feet or less being a realistic figure for the final phase of an attack. 'You might well fly the last few miles at fifty, but you can't keep that up all day, it's too exhausting.' If a Nimrod reconnaissance aircraft is in the vicinity, the formation relies on a VASTAC (Vector ASsisted TACtic) to locate the target. The VASTAC requires the Nimrod crew (flying at higher altitude) to pass the location details to the Buccaneers, thus avoiding any risk of the Buccaneers (which would otherwise have to use their own radars, and give away their location), being detected by enemy radar.

On the call of 'Bananas', our lead aircraft turns left and we turn right. They pull steeply into their climb, and we follow just four seconds later. The steep four g climb squeezes another sheet of condensation cloud over the wings and fuselage, and the climb develops into a roll, after the point at which the bombs would have been released.

Pulling smartly down to the horizon, the Spikers would now be illuminating a suitable spot on the side of an enemy warship, to which the bombs would relentlessly be heading. Meanwhile the LGB (laser-guided bomb) carriers drop back to the wave-tops to make good their escape. Although the Paveway is essentially a good-weather system (the bombs need to 'see' the illuminated target), it's a very effective means of destruction. It is important, however, that the target isn't 'Spiked' until the LGBs have reached the top of their launch trajectories, otherwise they will prematurely begin to home in towards the target without sufficient energy to get there (their toss climb takes roughly seventeen seconds). At about eight miles the two Spikers turn to present their port wings to the target and the navigators bring the laser beam on to target by means of a pistol grip and thumb wheel, and a TV screen. The camera head of the Pave Spike pod also provides a very useful visual recording of the attack, which can be replayed at debrief.

The Paveway system does require the aircraft to make fairly close approaches to the target, at ranges as short maybe as three miles. It is therefore very much a secondary means of attack for 208 Squadron, and their main offensive equipment is the BAeD P3T Sea Eagle sea-skimming missile; a 'fire-and-forget' weapon with all-weather day and night capability. There are many differing attack profiles practised by the Buccaneer crews, culminating in what is probably their most awesome deterrent; a six-ship 'Echo-One' Sea Eagle attack. In this profile, six Buccaneers each carry four Sea Eagles, flying line-abreast, less than 100 feet above the sea surface. A Nimrod provides a VASTAC or SURPIC (SURface PICture), giving basic area information on possible targets, or, if necessary, one Buccaneer briefly pulls up and designates a target. Once fed with the appropriate information, the 24-strong battery of missiles is released. The Sea Eagle is ECM (Electronic Counter Measures) resistant, and can be launched at distances in excess of 68 miles from the target. After firing their missiles, the Buccaneers turn through 180 degrees and depart, unseen by the enemy. Travelling at Mach 0.85, the missiles quickly close on the unsuspecting target ship: 'With a target like a Kirov class cruiser, there is a need to saturate the defences, but they can't pick off twenty-four missiles at once.' Total destruction is guaranteed, as the target vessel is virtually defenceless against these unseen assailants.

Heading back towards Lossiemouth, the Boss demonstrates a more warlike wave-top 'dash', dropping to 100 feet. The sea seems to rise and almost come into the cockpit, but over the sea the ride is still as smooth as glass. It's as good a demonstration of a Sea Eagle attack profile as one could get; there are no specific attack manoeuvres for launching this missile, as it is capable of turning into the target from virtually any position. During peacetime practice Sea Eagle attacks, the Buccaneer crews fly ASMD (Anti-Ship Missile Defence) profiles: 'We follow the kit to see where it leads us . . . we pretend actually to be the missiles.' Thus the unsuspecting target ship (usually belonging to the Royal Navy) gets an opportunity to train its gunners and missile operators with attacking aircraft; if the Buccaneers were doing this 'for real', though, they would never even be seen. Obviously the Buccaneer presents a much bigger target than the actual missile, and flies at a higher altitude (three metres being realistic for the Sea Eagle), but the approach speed can be imitated with precision, which gives the naval forces a useful training opportunity.

As the tower at Lossie gives the latest weather details, XV168 pulls into tight formation on our port wingtip, extending the large petal airbrakes which take six seconds to open fully. Their effect is most impressive, especially at high speed: 'like flying into a brick wall'. From a transit speed of 420 knots, we're suddenly down to an approach speed of 180 knots, as the landing gear slowly extends. The landing is almost always flown 'blown' (i.e. with Boundary Layer Control air pressure), and consequently the engine power is maintained at a fairly high setting in order to keep the high-pressure BLC in operation (speed being checked with the airbrakes). The control surfaces are brought down to their 45:25:25 positions (reflecting the corresponding instrument readings in the cockpit), and the Buccaneer assumes what is often referred to as 'marginally stable flight'. With typical aircrew understatement, this means that the Buccaneer is not, perhaps, the easiest of aircraft to handle in the airfield circuit, with lift directly dependent on the engine power. The Boss comments, 'She's not a happy aircraft with flaps and undercarriage down, on only one engine.' Fortunately the Buccaneer rarely needs to operate on one engine, as the Speys are remarkably reliable: 'The Speys are excellent . . . they eat birds and don't notice 'em.' As 'Skull One' turns on to finals ahead of 'Skull Two' and drops down on to the concrete, the second aircraft lines up on to approach. The ADD (Airstream Direction Detector) provides a visible and audible indication to the pilot of the aircraft's AOA (Angle of Attack). The navigator also hears the ADD through his helmet, and as the aircraft sinks on to the concrete the tone changes to a noise of protest — definitely not welcome unless the aircraft is firmly over the runway.

With a hefty thump, some three hours after departure, XT287 is back on the concrete. Already the ground crew will have been notified of our arrival, and they will be awaiting the aircraft's return at the HAS.

XV168 is already back in the squadron complex as we turn off the runway and on to the taxiway, our canopy sliding open to allow the welcome fresh air to flood the cockpit. The pins are all replaced in the ejection seat, apart from the face blind handle pin, which is out of reach (the ground crew will take care of this). The radar is switched off, having been used only briefly on this long flight, as the back-seater was preoccupied on this occasion with other matters; and in any case the subtleties of the display would doubtless have been lost on an untrained civilian's eye.

Back inside the HAS complex, the engines stop, the pilot and accompanying observer release their harnesses,

PECs and PSPs, untangle the leg restraints, unclip the RT leads, and confirm that the last pins are in place. The Boss stays in his 'office', while the ground crew connect a winch to the Buccaneer's fuselage and pull the aircraft backwards into the HAS, ready for refuelling and preparation for another sortie. Finally, crews return to the PBF to complete a speedy and informal debriefing, and the sortie is completed.

The Buccaneer is an old aircraft, but it still performs very effectively, and with its deadly Sea Eagles it presents a formidable prospect to any would-be aggressor. This capability, together with its Paveway equipment, makes its deployment by the RAF in the 1991 Gulf conflict a great deal less surprising.

The crews, of course, match the impressive capabilities of their aircraft, flying almost every day at high speed and low level over land and cold, lonely seas. They make the job look easy, but it is incredibly hard work. Pilots have flown into the water before, and others may well do so in the future. But the two-man Buccaneer crews take a philosophical attitude to the realities of their job, though the pilots and navigators certainly don't fool themselves that they are in the joy-riding business.

As a mere passenger, preparing to walk out to the Buccaneer and see for myself what it's all about, I was asked by a pilot: 'Are you nervous? No? Well, I always am when I'm going to do something dangerous.' Is it, in reality, a dangerous job? 'Well, I don't know — I suppose it is. Yes, it is dangerous; bloody dangerous!'

GLOSSARY

AAR	Air-to-Air Refuelling
ACE	Allied Command Europe
ACM	Air Combat Manoeuvring
ACT	Air Combat Training
Adex	Air Defence Exercise
ADD	Airstream Direction Detector
AIT	Air Intercept Trainer (Micro)
AMF	ACE Mobile Force
AMTC	Aviation Medicine Training Centre (North Luffenham)
AOA	Angle of Attack
APO	Acting Pilot Officer
ARA	Attack-Re-Attack
ASMD	Anti-Ship Missile Defence
ATC	Air Training Corps
BFTS	Basic Flying Training School
BLC	Boundary Layer Control
BMEWS	Ballistic Missile Early Warning System
CAP	Combat Air Patrol

151

CATO	Civil Air Traffic Operations
CCF	Combined Cadet Force
CEPT	Cockpit Emergency Procedure Trainer
CFS	Central Flying School (Scampton)
CINCUKAIR	Commander-in-Chief United Kingdom Air Forces
COMMAIREASTLANT	Commander Maritime Air Eastern Atlantic
COMMAIRCHAN	Commander Maritime Air Channel Command
Convex	Conversion Exercise
CP	Cadet Pilot
CPRO	Command Public Relations Officer
CRO	Community Relations Officer
CTTO	Central Trials and Tactics
DCN	Defence Communications Network
DIOT	Department of Initial Officer Training (Cranwell)
DNCO	Duty Not Carried Out
DS	Directing Staff
ECM	Electronic Counter Measures
EFATO	Engine Failure After Take Off
EFTS	Elementary Flying Training School (Swinderby)
FOB	Forward Operating Base
FHT	Final Handling Test
FSS	Flying Selection Squadron
FTS	Flying Training School
GH	General Handling
GST	General Service Training
HAS	Hardened Aircraft Shelter
HDU	Hose Drum Unit
IF	Instrument Flying
IFF	Identification Friend/Foe
ILS	Instrument Landing System
IOT	Initial Officer Training

IP	Initial Point
IRT	Instrument Rating Test
JFC	Joint Field Commander
LGB	Laser-Guided Bomb
MAMS	Mobile Air Movement Squadron
MATO	Military Air Traffic Operations
MDC	Miniature Detonating Cord
MOD	Ministry of Defence
MT	Motor Transport
MTA	Military Training Area
NADGE	Nato Air Defence Ground Environment
NATO	North Atlantic Treaty Organisation
NATS	National Air Traffic Services
Navex	Navigation Exercise
NBC	Nuclear Biological Chemical (Warfare)
NCO	Non-Commissioned Officer
OASC	Officers and Aircrew Selection Centre (Biggin Hill)
OCU	Operational Conversion Unit
PAR	Precision Approach Radar
PBF	Personal Briefing Facility
PEC	Personal Equipment Connector
PET	Practical Experience Training
PI	Practice Intercept
PMRAFNS	Princess Mary's RAF Nursing Service
PR	Photographic Reconnaissance
PSP	Personal Survival Pack
QFI	Qualified Flying Instructor
QRA	Quick Reaction Alert
QWI	Qualified Weapons Instructor
RCC	Rescue Co-ordination Centre (SAR)
RT	Radio Telephony
RV	Rendezvous
RWR	Radar Warning Receiver

SACEUR	Supreme Allied Commander Europe
SACLANT	Supreme Allied Commander Atlantic
SAM	Surface-to-Air Missile
SAP	Simulated Attack Profile
SAR	Search and Rescue
SLR	Single Lens Reflex camera
SNCO	Senior Non-Commissioned Officer
SOP	Standard Operating Procedure
SPILS	Spin Prevention and Incidence Limitation System
SRA	Surveillance Radar Approach
SSR	Secondary Surveillance Radar
SURPIC	Surface Picture
TACAN	Tactical Air Navigation equipment
TAIT	Tornado Airborne Intercept Trainer
TTTE	Tornado Tri-National Training Establishment (Cottesmore)
TWCU	Tornado Weapons Conversion Unit (Honington)
TWU	Tactical Weapons Unit
UAS	University Air Squadron
UNFICYP	United Nations Force in Cyprus
UPs	Unusual Positions
USAF	United States Air Force
VAs	Visual Aids
VASTAC	Vector Assisted Tactic
VW	Voluntary Withdrawal
WRAF	Women's Royal Air Force

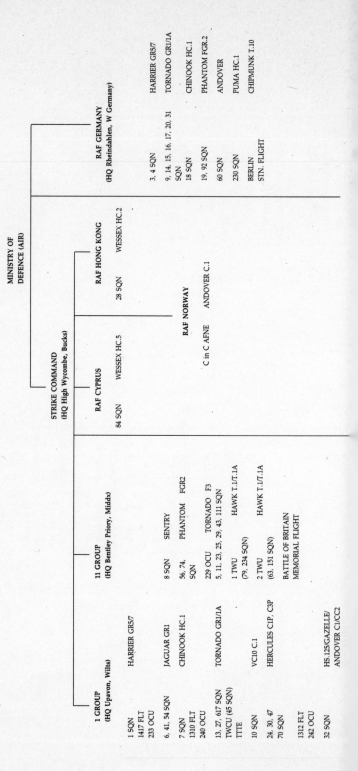

RAF COMMAND STRUCTURE 1991

MINISTRY OF
DEFENCE (AIR)

STRIKE COMMAND
(HQ High Wycombe, Bucks)

1 GROUP
(HQ Upavon, Wilts)

1 SQN	HARRIER GR5/7
1417 FLT	
233 OCU	
6, 41, 54 SQN	JAGUAR GR1
7 SQN	CHINOOK HC.1
1310 FLT	
240 OCU	
13, 27, 617 SQN	TORNADO GR1/1A
TWCU (45 SQN)	
TTTE	
10 SQN	VC10 C.1
24, 30, 47	HERCULES C1P, C3P
70 SQN	
1312 FLT	
242 OCU	
32 SQN	HS.125/GAZELLE/ ANDOVER C1/CC2

11 GROUP
(HQ Bentley Priory, Middx)

8 SQN	SENTRY
56, 74, SQN	PHANTOM FGR2
229 OCU	TORNADO F3
5, 11, 23, 25, 29, 43, 111 SQN	
1 TWU (79, 234 SQN)	HAWK T.1/T.1A
2 TWU (63, 151 SQN)	HAWK T.1/T.1A
BATTLE OF BRITAIN MEMORIAL FLIGHT	

RAF CYPRUS

84 SQN   WESSEX HC.5

RAF HONG KONG

28 SQN   WESSEX HC.2

RAF NORWAY

C in C AFNE   ANDOVER C.1

RAF GERMANY
(HQ Rheindahlen, W Germany)

3, 4 SQN	HARRIER GR5/7
9, 14, 15, 16, 17, 20, 31 SQN	TORNADO GR1/1A
18 SQN	CHINOOK HC.1
19, 92 SQN	PHANTOM FGR.2
60 SQN	ANDOVER
230 SQN	PUMA HC.1
BERLIN STN. FLIGHT	CHIPMUNK T.10

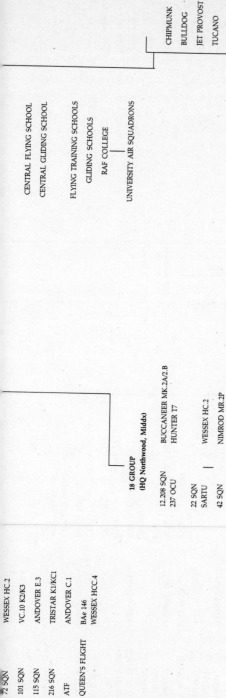

72 SQN — WESSEX HC.2
101 SQN — VC.10 K2/K3
115 SQN — ANDOVER E.3
216 SQN — TRISTAR K1/KC1
ATF — ANDOVER C.1
QUEEN'S FLIGHT — BAe 146 / WESSEX HCC.4

18 GROUP
(HQ Northwood, Middx)

12.208 SQN	BUCCANEER MK.2A/2.B
237 OCU	HUNTER T7
22 SQN SARTU	WESSEX HC.2
42 SQN	NIMROD MR 2P
51 SQN	NIMROD R.1P
100, 360 SQN No 1 PRU 231 OCU	CANBERRA
120, 201, 206 SQN 236 OCU	NIMROD MR.2P
202 SQN 1564 FLT SKTU	SEA KING HAR.3

CENTRAL FLYING SCHOOL
CENTRAL GLIDING SCHOOL

FLYING TRAINING SCHOOLS
GLIDING SCHOOLS
RAF COLLEGE
UNIVERSITY AIR SQUADRONS

CHIPMUNK
BULLDOG
JET PROVOST
TUCANO
HAWK
DOMINIE
JETSTREAM
GAZELLE
WESSEX

RAF COMMAND STRUCTURE 1991

STRIKE COMMAND

RAF Strike Command was formed on 30 April 1968, when two historic Commands, Bomber and Fighter, were merged. In addition, Signals and Coastal Commands were absorbed to become No. 90 (Signals) Group and No. 18 (Maritime) Group respectively. On 1 May 1972, No. 90 Group moved again to become part of Support Command. Finally, on 1 September 1972, Air Support Command amalgamated with Strike to form a single multi-role operational command.

The front line 'teeth' forces of the Royal Air Force in the United Kingdom are concentrated in Strike Command, which embraces the nuclear strike, conventional attack, reconnaissance, air defence, long-range maritime reconnaissance and air-to-air refuelling forces, together with certain calibration units, as well as those elements of air power required for the support of the Army in the field.

The almost complete integration of Strike Command within NATO was formally recognised on 10 April 1975, when the Air Officer Commanding-in-Chief was appointed a major subordinate commander under SACEUR with the Nato title of Commander-in-Chief United Kingdom Air Forces (CINCUKAIR). One of Strike Command's main responsibilities is for the United Kingdom Air Defence Region within which RAF fighters continue occasionally to intercept long-range Soviet aircraft.

Strike Command, with its headquarters at High Wycombe, Bucks, consists of three functional Groups in the UK and a regional Group in Cyprus, and is responsible for all overseas units except those in RAF Germany. These are No. 1 Group, which exercises day-to-day operational control and training of the strike/attack, ground attack, reconnaissance, support helicopter, air-to-air refuelling, air transport and RAF Regiment squadrons, the Tactical Communications Wing and the Queen's Flight; No. 11 Group, which similarly controls the air defence squadrons of Phantoms and their associated ground environment radars, including the Ballistic Missile Early Warning System at Fylingdales and the Bloodhound surface-to-air missile defences; and No. 18 Group with its responsibilities for long-range maritime reconnaissance, anti-submarine warfare and search and rescue. The Military Air Traffic Operations (MATO), with its headquarters at Uxbridge, is administered by Strike Command in peacetime and controlled by CINCUKAIR in war.

NO. 1 GROUP
The roles of No. 1 Group are the control and training in peacetime of all UK based strike/attack and tactical reconnaissance aircraft and tankers; the provision of offensive air support and helicopter support for the Army in the field; and the operation of strategic and tactical air transport forces which give air mobility to the Services. In wartime, most of the Group's resources are assigned to Nato.

STRIKE/ATTACK
The mainstay of Strike Command's strike/attack force is the Tornado force of No. 1 Group. The Tornado has

been in service since July 1980 at the Tornado Tri-national Training Establishment (TTTE) at RAF Cottesmore, where crews of the RAF, Italian Air Force, and German Air Force and Navy are given a conversion course. Weapons conversion for RAF crews takes place at the Tornado Weapons Conversion Unit (TWCU) at RAF Honington, and there are three UK based Tornado squadrons split between RAF Marham and RAF Honington.

TACTICAL SUPPORT

The Jaguar and Harrier provide offensive support and tactical reconnaissance, while the Puma, Wessex and heavy lift Chinook provide tactical and logistic support for the Army. These aircraft are earmarked for assignment to Nato in time of war, in support of the ACE Mobile Force (AMF), or for other theatre contingency plans.

AIR-TO-AIR REFUELLING (AAR)

The AAR fleet of Victor Mk 2 tankers will be phased out as VC10 K Mk 2/K Mk 3, and Tristar K Mk 1/KC Mk 2 tankers come into service. This re-equipment programme will both modernise No. 1 Group's tanker fleet and double its off-load capacity. No. 1 Group's tankers will continue to support RAF air defence, strike/attack, maritime patrol and tactical transport operations, wherever required, worldwide.

TRANSPORT

The long-range VC10s of No. 10 Squadron, Brize Norton, Oxford, can each carry 150 men in the operational trooping role, which means that an emergency lift of, say, 4000 men to Hong Kong could be completed by eight aircraft in about one week. On scheduled services the VC10s carry 125 passengers in airline comfort, whilst stripped of seats and furnishings they may also be used as freighters. Tristar aircraft, capable of operating in the freight and passenger role, will significantly increase the RAF's airlift capability and provide a strategic transport deployment capability over long ranges. The Tristar will be used primarily in the support of the British Forces in the Falkland Islands.

The Hercules, which has excellent range/payload capabilities, can be used in either a strategic or tactical role. The bulk carrying is being increased even more by the introduction of a stretched version.

While the transport force is frequently exercised at home and overseas with the Army and in support of RAF deployments, it is also productively employed in operation of scheduled air trooping and priority freight services. For this purpose staging facilities are established in the USA, Canada and at American bases in the Pacific for a Westabout route, as well as the more regularly used staging route via Cyprus to the Far East. No. 1 Group aircraft are also used as air ambulances. Patients, accompanied by flight sisters of Princess Mary's RAF Nursing Service and trained ambulance attendants, are flown home rapidly with the minimum of discomfort. There are regular VC10 'aeromedical' services from Hong Kong and Cyprus, and Hercules fly similar services from Germany and the Falkland Islands. The number of patients carried averages some 1500 per year.

OTHER TASKS

The Group also administers the Queen's Flight based at RAF Benson and trains parachutists of all three Services at No. 1 Parachute Training School at RAF Brize Norton. The instructors from this school form the 'Falcons', a free-fall demonstration team which performs at many European displays.

The UK based Light Armoured squadrons of the RAF Regiment and the depot at Catterick also belong to 1 Group. The Light Armoured squadrons are tasked with safeguarding RAF airfields and installations against ground attack, and are equipped with tracked combat vehicles, light mortars, short range anti-tank weapons and automatic weapons.

NO. 11 GROUP

No. 11 Group encompasses the UK Air Defence forces, the control and reporting organisation and the Royal Observer Corps. It is the Group's task to provide early warning of air attack against the United Kingdom Air Defences Region, to provide fighter and missile defences and the associated ground control system, fighter co-ordination with Royal Naval ships operating in adjacent waters and to maintain the integrity of UK airspace in war. The UK air defences form part of an integrated system under SACEUR. Although AOC-in-C Strike Command is the Regional Air Defence Commander, he delegates responsibility for day-to-day operational control to the AOC No. 11 Group.

AIR DEFENCE FORCES

The No. 11 Group Air Defence Squadrons are equipped with the Phantom FGR 2 and the Tornado F3, armed with Sky Flash and Sidewinder air-to-air missiles. In addition, the Hawk aircraft of No. 11 Group's two Tactical Weapons Units (TWU) at RAF Brawdy and RAF Chivenor have a day-fighter war role. Hawk aircraft are gun armed and capable of carrying Sidewinder. Further area defence is provided by Bloodhound Mk II surface-to-air missiles. Rapier missiles provide point defence. Shackleton AEW Mk II aircraft operating from the North of Scotland have provided Airborne Early Warning and control for interceptors for a number of years. However, the Shackleton has now been replaced by the Boeing Sentry aircraft. Low level air defence of airfields is provided by Rapier-equipped Air Defence squadrons of the RAF Regiment. In addition, an Auxiliary Squadron has been formed, equipped with Oerlikon and Skyguard.

CONTROL AND REPORTING

The control and reporting system consists of a chain of powerful radar stations from the Faeroes to Southern England. These are linked with other elements of the NATO Air Defence Ground Environment (NADGE) and with the Ballistic Missile Early Warning Systems

163

(BMEWS) station at Fylingdales, Yorkshire, which is net-worked with the US-operated BMEWS at Thule (Green-land) and Clear (Alaska). By extending high-level radar cover some 3000 miles across Eastern Europe, Fylingdales would give advance warning of intermediate range ballis-tic missiles launched against the UK and Western Europe, and of inter-continental ballistic missiles against the North American continent. Fylingdales also tracks satel-lites and space debris.

ROYAL OBSERVER CORPS

The Home Office is responsible, through the United King-dom Warning and Monitoring Organisation, for the oper-ational policy and operational control of the Royal Observer Corps, while the commandant is responsible to the Ministry of Defence for the administrative efficiency of the corps.

The Royal Observer Corps is equipped and trained to report nuclear bursts and forecast fall-out levels, infor-mation which would be passed to the Home Defence organisation and controlling military HQs.

NO. 18 GROUP

No. 18 Group provides a major element of Britain's mari-time forces and, with the Royal Navy and Nato allies, is responsible for the safety of sea communications in the Atlantic, North Sea and home waters. With its long-range Nimrod maritime reconnaissance aircraft, the Group has the paramount peacetime task of carrying out surveillance operations to maintain a flow of information about the movements of potentially hostile surface vessels and sub-marines over ocean areas.

The main activities of the Group are maritime surface and subsurface surveillance, search and rescue (SAR) and regular patrolling of the North Sea oil and gas instal-lations, and fishery limits. Tasks are controlled from the Air Headquarters at Northwood, Middlesex. In war, the Nimrods would operate under the Supreme Allied Com-mander Atlantic (SACLANT), the AOC No. 18 Group holding the Nato posts of Commander Maritime Air Eastern Atlantic (COMMAIREASTLANT) and Commander Maritime Air Channel Command (COMMAIRCHAN). As such, his main tasks would be to provide maritime strike/-attack, maritime reconnaissance and anti-submarine support for naval operations and in protection of allied merchant shipping.

The Nimrod is a turbo jet maritime patrol aircraft and is considered to be among the world's most effective submarine killers. The Nimrod Mk I first entered service with Strike Command in October 1969, and has now been replaced by the Nimrod Mk 2, which has a better communications fit, a more advanced radar called Searchwater, a new acoustic processor employing digital techniques to handle data from two new types of sonar buoy, a new inertial navigation system and a more sophisticated computer. Nimrod squadrons are based at RAF Kinloss in Scotland and RAF St Mawgan in Cornwall. However, the primary land-based maritime strike/attack aircraft is the Buccaneer which carries Martel and Sea Eagle stand-off air-to-surface missiles.

No. 18 Group controls SAR through the Rescue Co-ordination Centres at Plymouth and Edinburgh. The Group's search and rescue Sea King and Wessex helicopters with, where appropriate, the Nimrods and marine craft units, are frequently engaged in rescue work and mercy flights, saving several hundred lives each year.

RECONNAISSANCE

No. 18 Group is also responsible for photographic reconnaissance cover using Canberra PR9. The Canberra PR unit also undertakes photographic surveys for the Ministry of Defence and other government departments in many parts of the world.

OVERSEAS BASES

Strike Command has responsibility for all RAF bases overseas with the exception of those administered by HQ RAF Germany. There are units in the Mediterranean, Far East, North America and Central America.

AHQ Cyprus has Group status within Strike Command. In Cyprus, there is a resident squadron of Wessex helicopters, some of which support UNFICYP with the remainder in the SAR role, while facilities exist at RAF Akrotiri to support aircraft detached from UK. In addition, an RAF Regiment Squadron is deployed at Akrotiri for airfield defence.

RAF Gibraltar is directly administered by HQ 18 Group. The airfield is operated by the RAF, although there is no resident squadron.

Strike Command controls RAF units for administrative and engineering purposes in Hong Kong where there is a squadron of Wessex helicopters.

In North America there is a Strike Command detachment at Offutt Air Force Base, Nebraska, to support overseas training detachments, and a permanent unit is established at Goose Bay in Labrador for a similar purpose.

There is also a permanent 1 Group detachment of Harriers, Puma helicopters, and a Rapier Air Defence Unit in Belize. Strike Command also provides a Phantom Air Defence flight, a flight of Hercules transport/tankers and Sea King and Chinook helicopters in the Falkland Islands.

During operations and exercises, 1 Group aircraft often visit overseas airfields where no regular RAF ground handling organisation exists. For this purpose at RAF Lyneham the Group has a Mobile Air Movement Squadron (MAMS) which provides teams who are expert in all aspects of loading and unloading aircraft.

These MAMS teams log a large number of flying hours annually and are normally on the first aircraft in and last aircraft out in any major overseas operation, exercise or relief operation.

MILITARY AIR TRAFFIC OPERATIONS
Military Air Traffic Operations (MATO) has Group status within Strike Command and is based at Hillingdon House, Uxbridge. It is co-located with Civil Air Traffic Operations (CATO) under a Joint Field Commander (JFC), who is responsible for the joint implementation of National Air Traffic Services (NATS) policy for the control of civil and military aircraft in the UK.

AOC MATO is operationally responsible to the Controller NATS for all military ATC services in UK airspace other than those provided at airfields.

CENTRAL TRIALS AND TACTICS ORGANISATION

The Central Trials and Tactics Organisation (CTTO) is responsible for formulating tactical doctrine and conducting operational trials. It also maintains liaison with MOD research establishments and industry, and close contact with RAF operational commands and with the Royal Navy, Army and Allied air forces.

The CTTO is located at and administered by HQ Strike Command, but is responsible jointly to the Assistant Chief of Air Staff and to the Commander-in-Chief for the conduct of trials and development of tactics for all Royal Air Force operational aircraft.

RAF GERMANY

This Command sprang directly from the forces designed to exploit the air weapon over Europe in World War Two. Its origins go back to the Second Tactical Air Force, a British formation created to provide support for the allied invasion of the continent, a task it fulfilled with great success from D Day to VE Day. At the end of the war it became the British Air Force of Occupation but reverted to its former title after a few years. Then in 1959 it was renamed RAF Germany.

From the start, therefore, the Command was geared to operate in a European environment and it is now more closely integrated than any other part of the Royal Air Force into the structure of NATO. Its Commander-in-Chief is ex officio Commander of the Second Allied Tactical Air Force, a NATO organisation activated in 1952 (2ATAF, as opposed to the wholly British 2TAF), whose members also include West Germany, the United States, Belgium and Holland.

The air forces of these five nations cover an immense area of responsibility, some 60,000 square miles of land

and sea between the old Inner German Border and the Franco-Belgian border. Their aircraft, in addition to exercising regularly together to co-ordinate tactics and training, land at each other's airfields to allow ground-crew to become proficient in cross-servicing different types.

The contribution made by RAF Germany embraces the whole range of missions that would be carried out in war: counter-air, interdiction, ground attack, reconnaissance, air defence and tactical helicopter operations.

Counter-air (that is, attacks on enemy airfields, radar stations and SAM sites) and interdiction (attacks on choke points along enemy lines of communication to hinder the forward movement of reinforcements and supplies) fall to the Tornado GR1. The advent of this aircraft was hailed by the Commander-in-Chief at the time as a quantum jump in capability. 'It gives us for the first time the ability to penetrate enemy defences at high speed and very low level by day or night and in virtually any weather and attack key targets with great accuracy,' he said.

Direct support of the Army is carried out by the Harrier GR5 and GR7, unique weapons in NATO's armoury. Its short take-off and vertical landing capability enable it to operate from dispersed sites close to the battlefield which means that its sortie rate is superior to that of any other allied warplane. Harriers equip Nos. 3 and 4 Squadrons at Gutersloh, a former Luftwaffe airfield.

Also at Gutersloh is the Support Helicopter Force, the Chinooks of 18 Squadron and Pumas of 230 Squadron, both dedicated to the back-up of 1 BR Corps, the front-line element of BAOR. As a general workhorse the heli-copter has revolutionised the logistic support of forces in the field and made possible the development of new air-mobile tactics.

The air defence element of RAF Germany currently comprises two squadrons of Spey-engined Phantom FGR2 aircraft stationed at RAF Wildenrath. With recent changes in the political status of Germany, the RAF will soon withdraw from Wildenrath, the Phantoms returning to England, and a Tornado F3 unit moving into Germany to join other Luftwaffe (and former East German airforce) aircraft in the air defence of Germany.

Airfield defence against low-flying aircraft is provided by four RAF Regiment squadrons equipped with Rapier surface-to-air missiles and Blindfire radar. Other Regiment squadrons with Scorpion and Spartan armoured vehicles contribute to the ground defence of main bases and deployed Harrier forces. RAF Germany, with headquarters at Rheindahlen near Monchengladbach, controls the RAF Hospital at Wegberg and maintains a Support Unit at Decimomannu, a NATO base in Sardinia, where units go regularly for air combat and weapons training.

RAF SUPPORT
COMMAND STRUCTURE

Royal Air Force Support Command was formed in June 1977 by the merger of Training and Support Commands. It has its headquarters at RAF Brampton, near Huntingdon in Cambridgeshire. The merger brought together all those elements which in the past had formed Flying Training, Technical Training, Maintenance and Signals Commands and gave the RAF a three-Command structure; Strike Command and RAF Germany with the 'teeth', and RAF Support Command.

RAF Support Command is responsible for flying training and the training of officers and airmen in ground branches and trades; the provision of communications, supply and movements facilities; those deeper electrical and mechanical engineering functions which are beyond the capacity of stations; the hospitals and specialist medical units in the UK, and many administrative services throughout the RAF. To undertake these diverse tasks, the Command has two functional groups — Training and Maintenance — embedded in the Command Headquarters, together with the RAF College at Cranwell, the RAF Staff College at Bracknell and HQ Air Cadets at Newton.

The total strength of the Command is approximately 47,000, which includes about 12,000 civilians and typically some 8000 to 8500 men and women under training. The main work of the Command is undertaken at 64 units on 42 stations.

TRAINING

RAF Support Command is responsible for the basic training and most of the trade, refresher and staff training of officers and airmen. The tasks include initial training on entry to the Service, aircrew training and the specialist training of ground branch officers and airmen in ground trades. In addition, many types of training are provided for personnel of Commonwealth and foreign air forces and for other government departments.

INITIAL OFFICER TRAINING

On entry to the Royal Air Force, all potential officers undergo initial Officer Training at the RAF College Cranwell. They are then commissioned and, unless they are already professionally qualified (for example as doctors or dentists), are given specialist training on the ground or in the air.

Those potential officers who are RAF University Cadets become members of one of the sixteen University Air Squadrons (UASs). The UASs, which are controlled by the RAF College Cranwell, aim to encourage the cadets' motivation and development as junior officers. They administer and supervise the cadets, provide ab initio flying training for those entering as pilots or navigators and give flying experience for those going to other branches.

FLYING TRAINING

After Initial Officer Training, potential pilots with no significant previous flying experience go to the Elementary Flying Training School at RAF Swinderby in Lincolnshire, where their suitability to proceed to basic flying training is assessed and developed. Basic flying training is then given on Jet Provost or Tucano aircraft at one of the Command's Flying Training Schools, and at the end of that course the students are selected for one of three streams for advanced training up to 'Wings' standard: fast-jet pilots for air defence and ground attack squadrons, whose training continues on Hawk aircraft; those destined for squadrons with multi-engined aircraft like Nimrod or Hercules train on the Jetstream; and training for rotary wing aircraft is undertaken on the Gazelle and Wessex. All navigators are trained in Dominie and Jet Provost aircraft at both high and low level.

At the end of a basic phase, they are streamed for fast-jet or multi-engined aircraft and their advanced training then has a strong bias to low or high level as appropriate.

For all airmen aircrew entering the RAF, the Command provides an Initial Training Course similar to that for officers. The Sergeant Air Engineers and Air Electronic Operators then train alongside the navigators on Dominie aircraft, whilst the helicopter crewmen train beside the pilots on the Wessex.

In addition to this all-through flying training, the Command provides a twenty-week primary fixed-wing flying course on Bulldog aircraft for all naval pilots, and refresher training for RAF aircrew who are returning to flying after a tour of duty in a ground appointment.

Flying instructors for all three Services and for a number of overseas countries as well are trained at the Central Flying School (CFS), the oldest flying training school in the world. CFS also provides the RAF Aerobatic Team, the Red Arrows.

GROUND TRAINING

The Command maintains a number of schools for ground training. At some, officers and airmen train together, but, where possible, officer training is undertaken at the RAF College Cranwell. There are specialist courses for those being commissioned in engineering, supply, air-traffic control, secretarial, catering, physical eduction, police

175

and education, and orientation courses for doctors, dentists and padres. The same facilities are used to provide courses to update or extend their expertise as they progress through the Service and their responsibilities widen.

For the new airmen and airwomen, the Command provides six weeks' basic training at the Recruit Training School. They then go for specialist training in any one of about 150 separate trades which are themselves divided into nineteen main groups. By far the largest part of that training task is concerned with engineering tradesmen who need to be expert on complex aircraft, electrical and electronic systems, modern instrumentation, automatic test equipment, radar and radio, propulsion units, weapon systems and all types of ground vehicles.

In addition, men and women must be trained to operate these equipments, to be medical and dental assistants, communications specialists, and to be part of modern supply management and administration, often involving the extensive use of computers. As with officers, the initial training needs to be supplemented at later stages in the trademen's careers. All told, about 25,000 servicemen and women pass through the courses at the various Schools of Training in the Command each year.

In addition, because of its large number of civilian employees, the Command has technical training schools where civilian employees learn basic and specialist engineering skills and a small number of craftsmen are trained as apprentices. The Command also gives management and administrative training to civilians in the junior and middle grades of management.

Altogether, RAF Support Command provides over 600 different ground training courses. These courses can vary greatly, from a week or so to show a qualified typist how the Service does things, to three years for RAF Apprenticeships. Many courses are devised to meet particular and changing needs as new equipments are brought into use. In addition, on behalf of the RAF, the command carries out General Service Training and Trade Management Training for airmen and airwomen selected for promotion to corporal and for corporals selected for promotion to sergeant. The aim is to ensure that they are better qualified for their new role and responsibilities.

COMMAND AND STAFF TRAINING

The fundamental requirements of an RAF officer are professional competence in his specialist role and executive ability. However, as he advances in rank, he is expected to assume wider responsibilities and command, and staff training is designed to develop this breadth. The RAF Staff College provides an Officers' Command Course for officers who have served for some years. This is followed by the Individual Staff Studies course which lasts eighteen months and is conducted as a correspondence course. These officers are then qualified for the Basic Staff Course at Bracknell after which, as Squadron Leaders or Wing Commanders, they can be selected to attend the Advanced Staff Course, which gives them a firm grounding on which to go forward to the higher levels of the Service.

AIR CADETS

The Air Officer Commanding Air Cadets is also the Commandant of the ATC, in which role he is responsible for some 45,000 young men in about 1000 units throughout the UK. As Air Officer Commanding Air Cadets, he provides, within RAF Support Command, air experience flying and gliding for the various ATC Wings, using thirteen Air Experience Flights and twenty-seven Gliding Schools spread across the UK.

MAINTENANCE SUPPORT

The maintenance functions of RAF Support Command can be divided into those engineering functions connected with aircraft together with their weapons (Aerosystems Maintenance), Communications together with Ground Electronics (Signals) and Supply and Movements.

AEROSYSTEMS ENGINEERING

RAF Support Command provides aircraft engineering support in the form of scheduled major servicing, rectification, reconditioning and modification of a wide variety of fixed-wing aircraft for the RAF, the Royal Navy and the Army Air Corps. The ability of RAF Support Command to turn round aircraft quickly and to accept urgent tasks at short notice is of great importance both in operational and economic terms, because the high cost of modern aircraft restricts the number that can be bought and therefore requires that they should be serviceable in the front line for as much of their Service life as possible.

The Aircraft Engineering Units of the Command service or repair most of the aircraft in the RAF inventory, including major servicing tasks on Harrier, Buccaneer, Victor, Phantom, Tornado, Jaguar, Hunt and Hawk aircraft, as well as Sea Harriers and communications aircraft for the Royal Navy. They also handle about half of the repair work arising on the Adour engines fitted in the Jaguar and Hawk and on the RB 199 engines in the Tornado, plus a proportion of mechanical and structural component arisings. Advanced and sophisticated aircraft production techniques are used and these, coupled with the employment of network analysis backed up by computers as a means of planning the complex task of aircraft servicing, enable the Service and civilian workforce to achieve a high peacetime level of responsiveness and efficiency whilst developing and maintaining the essential skills needed for immediate support of the front line in war.

In modern combat aircraft, avionics are increasingly important and the Command provides a direct exchange and loan repair scheme for the avionics and some guided weapon equipment in use throughout the RAF so as to minimise the loss of flying time in front-line squadrons. Speed of exchange is of the essence and this service is also provided to a number of Navy, Army and Ministry of Defence (MOD) research stations in the UK. The Command has the workshops, production lines and test facilities to service over 80,000 items of avionic equipment a year.

Within the Command, a Repair and Salvage Squadron is responsible for salvaging crashed aircraft worldwide for both the MOD and the Department of Trade. It also sends teams of tradesmen to operational stations to undertake aircraft modifications and repairs which are beyond the capacity of unit personnel, but which do not require the aircraft to be returned to industry. It also has responsibility for devising repair techniques for dealing with battle damage and provides formal training in these techniques to the other Services and, on occasions, Allied Forces.

In addition to the major aircraft engineering task, RAF Support Command has the capability to undertake the modification, repair and servicing of almost any item held in Supply Depots or returned in an unserviceable condition from units whenever it is expedient and economical to do so. The facilities are economic since they obviate the need for additional back-up spares of expensive equipment and allow for an unpredicted demand for scarce equipment to be met quickly. The Command also provides in situ maintenance facilities for medical and dental equipment in support of the RAF hospitals at home and overseas and a repair and calibration service for over 72,000 items of test equipment per annum.

SUPPLY AND MOVEMENTS

The supply task of RAF Support Command is in two parts, which may be likened to the retail and wholesale functions of commerce. Retail activity involves the day to day provision of the whole range of supply support for the Command's disparate stations and for the flying training fleet of over 460 aircraft, together with its many and varied engineering commitments in the maintenance area. For this purpose, a Supply and Movements organisation is established on each of our stations to account for and control all stocks.

On the wholesale side, the Command provides a complete functional supply service, including the control and distribution from the repair and storage depots to the customer for the RAF worldwide and, for air stores and accommodation stores, for the Royal Navy and Army. For this work, the Command has a number of storage units, including large supply depots, ammunition and compressed gas storage depots and petroleum supply depots. All told, these units hold about 1,230,000 different types of technical and domestic equipment; the amounts of each vary from a few months' stock to sufficient for several years, depending on whether the item can be replenished quickly or can be bought in economic quantities only when the manufacturer is tooled to produce it. Because of the highly technical nature of the equipment and aircraft in our Service and the need for operational reaction and resilience, the stock is greater, and the variety wider, than could be found in any one civilian firm in the UK.

The ability to provide a particular item when it is needed may directly affect the serviceability of an operational aircraft or facility, so emphasis is placed on stock recording, stock location, speed of handling and timely distribution throughout the movements network. Today, the highest priority demands for equipment are fully processed within a few hours of their receipt at the depot via a real-time, on-line computer driven stock control system which links all stations, depots, provisioning and command staffs. This system operates 24 hours a day, every day of the year.

SIGNALS

The signals responsibilities of RAF Support Command fall into four main categories: Telecommunications, Signals Engineering, Ground Radio Repair and Avionic Installation.

In the Telecommunications field, the Command is responsible for operating the RAF element of the Defence Communications Network (DCN). For strategic communications, the Command is the sole system and engineering design authority for the DCN worldwide. It also acts as a consultant to MOD, other RAF Commands and to Commonwealth and Allied Air Forces for all aspects of communications.

The operating responsibilities divide into three categories. First, there is a complex of high frequency transmitters and receivers in the UK, providing services to the DCN, Strike Command and the Meteorological Office. The Command also maintains and operates signals message relay centres: a small residual element of manual signals processing remains, but the vast majority of signals traffic is now processed using computer controlled automatic message routing. Finally, the Command operates and maintains the control centre for the Skynet satellite communications system, which provides high quality speech, telegraph and data links, both strategic and tactical, for all three Services.

The second category of Signals activity is Signals Engineering, and the Command has the capability to design, manufacture and install communications and radar equipment. This facility does not replace industry but complements it. Standard commercial items of equipment are frequently integrated with RAF designed and manufactured interfaces into one-off systems precisely tailored to the Services' needs.

The Command also has the facilities and expertise for the deep repair of a large proportion of the RAF's Electrical Installations, Air Defence Radars, Point-to-Point and Ground-to-Air Communications and Radio aids to navigation. The Command assists the operational units to maintain such equipment in use, particularly where this involves regular flight performance checking (e.g. for radars, navigation and approach aids) and undertaking major routine servicing and repair.

Finally, the Command maintains an Avionic Installation engineering capability and the expertise to enable quick reaction assistance to be provided to the front line. In this field, the staff work particularly closely with the Operational Commands and the work is carried out under the Service Radio Installation Modifications.

ADMINISTRATIVE SUPPORT
An important element of the administrative support which the Command provides to the Service as a whole

is the RAF hospitals in the United Kingdom as well as several specialist medical units. The Command also provides facilities for medical evacuation by air and investigates the medical aspects of aircraft accidents worldwide.

More generally, and apart from the routine administration of its 64 functional units, the Command provides administrative support for some 148 other units in the UK and abroad. These include the men and women in the RAF Careers Information Offices, embassy staffs, liaison staffs on the American bases in this country, those in the Central Band of the Royal Air Force, the servicemen working in MOD (Procurement Executive) establishments, such as Farnborough, and those working in the Air Force Department itself.

THE FUTURE

It is in the nature of a Service which operates in many respects on the frontiers of technology that the demands it places on its men, women and equipment continually increase. As the skills which are needed vary, and the techniques of production and repair change, the continuing task of RAF Support Command is to provide the materiel and the trained men and women needed to support the front line in peace and war in the most cost-effective and efficient way possible. Hence the motto on the Command badge: *Ut Aquilae Volent* — 'That Eagles May Fly'.

RESCUE FROM THE SKIES

The RAF's Search and Rescue service provides all-year round emergency cover for those in peril at sea and on land. Although primarily intended as a military emergency service, the majority of SAR work involves civilian incidents. This has led to the sight of a yellow helicopter becoming as familiar as the coastguard and RNLI lifeboat organisation to the British public. The organisation consists of three units, the Rescue Co-ordination Centres (RCCs), the flying units and the mountain rescue teams.

Two RCCs, one at Pitreavie Castle, Dunfermline, and the other at Mount Wise, Plymouth, are responsible for co-ordinating calls for assistance and the subsequent rescue operations.

The flying units consist of four aircraft types. The Nimrod maritime patrol aircraft and Shackleton airborne early warning aircraft can be used to search for survivors and give guidance assistance to rescue craft and helicopters at the scene of the incident. They can also be used to drop survival equipment and liferafts if needed. Four Sea King helicopter flights and five Wessex helicopter flights are evenly distributed around the coast of the United Kingdom to provide maritime and land rescue cover. Each flight is on 24-hour standby, 365 days a year. The Wessex has a range of 90 nautical miles and the capacity to carry fourteen survivors. It has a three-man crew (pilot, navigator and winchman).

The Sea King is one of the most capable search and rescue helicopters in current service. It has an automatic flight control system enabling transition from forward flight to an automatic doppler hover. Used in conjunction with its homing aids and radar, it enables a full instrument recovery to be made, giving it a true all-weather capability. The aircraft has a radius of action of 280 nautical miles and the carrying capacity for eighteen survivors. The crew of four consists of two pilots, a radar/winch operator and a winchman.

In August 1984, the Royal Air Force completed one of the world's longest helicopter rescue missions when a Brawdy-based Sea King, from South Wales, recovered an injured seaman from a cargo vessel some 400 miles into the Atlantic, southwest of the Irish Republic. The nine-hour flight involved refuelling stops in Southern Ireland and the offshore drilling platform, Glomer Arctic.

The final, but by no means least important unit of the RAF SAR service is provided by the six Mountain Rescue teams covering the mountainous areas of the United Kingdom. Each team, comprising about 30 men, is equipped with suitable vehicles and a comprehensive range of climbing and rescue equipment. The men are all highly dedicated, and give up large amounts of their spare time for training. As a result, each team is made up of highly skilled mountaineers who know their local area very well, and are on one hour's notice all year round. Often they work with the SAR helicopters to conclude successfully what would be an impossible task for a helicopter alone, particularly in bad weather.

The RAF Search and Rescue service is now a well established national asset, and is likely to remain one of the most visible components of the armed Services in the public eye.

THE RAF REGIMENT

The need to raise a dedicated specialist force to protect air installations became apparent during World War Two when unprotected aircraft on the ground were vulnerable to enemy air and ground attack. Consequently the RAF Regiment was raised on 1 February 1942 by a Royal Warrant of King George VI. The RAF Regiment was to be, and remains, a Corps within the Royal Air Force. Her Majesty Queen Elizabeth II is the Corps Air Commodore-in-Chief.

The RAF Regiment exists to provide ground defence and short range air defence for RAF installations and to train all RAF combatant personnel so that they can contribute to the defence of their unit. To this end the RAF Regiment maintains six Light Armoured Squadrons equipped with the Combat Vehicle Reconnaissance (Tracked) (CVR(T)) and six Short Range Air Defence Squadrons equipped with the Rapier system, to meet the ground and low level air defence threats respectively. Additionally, the RAF Regiment mans three further Rapier Squadrons specifically raised to provide the short range air defence for USAF bases in UK. A recent innovation has been the formation of seven Royal Auxiliary Air Force Regiment squadrons, six of which are field squadrons and one of which is an air defence squadron equipped with the Skyguard system captured from the Argentinians during the Falklands War.

Each Light Armoured Squadron is organised into flights, equipped with Sultan Armoured Command Posts, Samson Armoured Reconnaissance Vehicles and Spartan Armoured Personnel Carriers. Light Armoured Squadron are based in the UK, Germany and Cyprus.

In the air defence role the six Rapier squadrons are all equipped with the Blindfire radar giving them an all-weather day and night capability. Four squadrons are based in RAF Germany under the command of 4 Wg RAF Regt and the other two are UK-based under the command of the AOC 11 Gp. The UK-based Rapier squadrons maintain a detachment in Belize to protect the RAF Harriers, helicopters and the international airport. The Rapier squadrons from RAF Germany provide, on rotation, the short range air defence for Mount Pleasant Airfield in the Falkland Islands. The Royal Auxiliary Air Force Regiment units are a recent addition to the Corps. They consist of 155 all ranks of which 85 per cent are locally recruited auxiliaries. These squadrons provide dedicated ground defence support for specific airfields and are equipped with soft-skinned vehicles, small-arms, machine guns, light mortars and light anti-armour weapons. One of the auxiliary squadrons is equipped with the Skyguard anti-aircraft system and provides short range air defence for a UK base. The Regiment is not alone in defending any RAF station. Every airman based at a station has a ground defence role. He is trained to defend his place of work against ground attack, and defend it even though it may be under attack by NBC weapons. He has been trained in these skills by the RAF Regiment. Every officer or airman posted to a station is allocated these tasks and will be given a series of courses in various aspects of ground defence by RAF Regiment instructors. The provision of these training courses is an important part of the duties of the RAF Regiment.

The RAF Regiment Depot at Catterick is responsible for the basic training of all officers and gunners. On completion of his eighteen-week initial officer training at the RAF College Cranwell, the RAF Regiment officer is commissioned and reports to RAF Catterick for his initial specialist and role training. Many of the skills that he has developed at Cranwell will stand him in good stead but he will find the Junior Regiment Officer's Course more strenuous, demanding and challenging than the training that he has so far undertaken. The course lasts 22 weeks and gives the junior officer a firm grounding in fundamental tactics and fieldcraft. He learns to handle different infantry weapons and conduct live range firing practices, and acquires the skills of map reading, first aid and the administration of a unit in the field. Battlecraft camps are held on the bleak moors of North Yorkshire. On qualifying he will be posted to an operational RAF Regiment squadron for his first tour where he will practise his newly learnt skills.

Exchange schemes allow the RAF Regiment officer to serve with other forces throughout the world and it is significant that many forces have modelled their own airfield defence policy on the RAF Regiment. In this country RAF Regiment personnel can be found at the School of Infantry at Warminster, at Royal Marines Commando and the RAF Staff College.

Besides the provision of specialist squadrons and ground defence training instructors at RAF stations, the RAF Regiment has several other tasks. RAF Regiment instructors serve at all major formal RAF training establishments and at the joint-service Defence NBC Centre. Additionally the RAF Regiment mans the Queen's Colour Squadron which undertakes all major ceremonial duties for the Royal Air Force. These duties involve mounting the guard at Buckingham Palace on an occasional basis and providing guards of honour for visiting heads of state. The Queen's Colour Squadron is also well known for its continuity drill displays where complex drill movements are performed without words of command. The Queen's Colour Squadron has a war role in support of RAF assets in RAF Germany.

The expertise of the Regiment has recently been acknowledged by the memorandum of understanding, in which the USAF has undertaken to buy Rapier missile systems to defend seven bases in the UK. The Rapiers will be manned by RAF Regiment and RAF personnel (at US expense). Another Wing Headquarters has been formed to command the squadrons, which are organised, trained and equipped to normal RAF Regiment standards.

Command of operational units and training staffs is exercised through normal RAF channels. Squadrons, therefore, are under the operational command of their respective AOC or CinC. Further operational and training requirements and policy are determined by the Commandant-General RAF Regiment and his staff at the Ministry of Defence.

PRINCESS MARY'S RAF
NURSING SERVICE

The Royal Air Force Nursing Service was formed on 1 June 1918, and by the end of that year numbered 42 nursing sisters. Although they held officer status, they were known by their professional titles.

In June 1923, His Majesty King George V gave the Royal Assent for the RAF Nursing Service to be known as Princess Mary's Royal Air Force Nursing Service. Her Royal Highness Princess Mary, later the Princess Royal, became their first Air Chief Commandant.

With the outbreak of hostilities in 1939 the Service was enlarged. During World War Two the nursing sisters served in hospitals in Iraq, Palestine, Benghazi, Cairo, Iceland, West Africa, India, the Bahamas and Japan. Additionally, they served in mobile field hospitals in Burma, Singapore, the Western Desert, Italy, France, the Netherlands, Algiers, the North African coast, Sicily and Sardinia. The sisters also worked in the sick bays of troop ships and casualty reception areas, and played their part in casualty evacuation flights.

189

After the war, casualty air evacuation, renamed aero-medical evacuation, was further developed and members of the PMRAFNS participated in the evacuation of casualties from both the Korean War and the Malayan Emergency.

In 1966, Her Majesty The Queen appointed Her Royal Highness Princess Alexandra, The Hon. Mrs Angus Ogilvy, as Royal Patron and Air Chief Commandant of the PMRAFNS.

Today, members of the PMRAFNS serve at three RAF hospitals in the UK (Ely, Halton and Wroughton) and overseas in Cyprus and Germany. A few nursing officers serve elsewhere abroad including Islamabad, Peking and Sek Kong. Enrolled Nurses (General) also have the opportunity to serve at Medical Centres within the UK and overseas in Gibraltar, Belize, Ascension Island, the Falklands and some Nato posts.

Currently there are three methods of entry into the PMRAFNS: first, as commissioned officers with Registered Nurse qualification and at least one year's post-registered experience; secondly, as a direct entrant holding the Enrolled Nurse (General) qualification in non-commissioned rank; and thirdly, as pupil nurses, to train as Enrolled Nurse (General) at Wroughton or Ely.

Prior to 1980, the PMRAFNS had its own rank structure and was restricted to female nursing officers and nurses, but on 1 April 1980, when the Royal Air Force Unified Nursing Service was inaugurated, the PMRAFNS became a complete nursing service. All male registered and enrolled nurses were now members of the PMRAFNS, resulting in equal opportunities for promotion to top level posts for commissioned officers, and to the rank of Warrant Officer for airmen/women.

The PMRAFNS is fully integrated in the Royal Air Force. Nursing Officers hold the Queen's Commission, use rank titles and complete either Short Service Commissions or enjoy a full career with a permanent commission.

THE WOMEN'S
ROYAL AIR FORCE

The Women's Royal Air Force came into existence on 1
April 1918, with elements of the Women's Auxiliary Army
Corps and Women's Royal Naval Service already serving
with the air units of the Army and Navy being offered a
transfer to the new Service.

During its brief two-year life the WRAF boasted 32,000
members, until it was disbanded in 1920.

It was to be nineteen years before it was re-formed. The
initial steps were taken in 1938 when, with war clouds
gathering over Europe, the Imperial Defence Committee
changed its policy of not recruiting women for the Services in times of peace. The result was the signing of a
Royal Warrant on 9 September heralding the Auxiliary
Territorial Service. By 28 June 1939, just under three
months before the start of World War Two, 48 RAF Com-
panies of the ATS transferred to form the nucleus of the
new Women's Auxiliary Air Force (WAAF). With less
than 2000 women in one officer branch and six trades,

the Service expanded until, by mid-1943, nearly 182,000 women were serving in 22 officer branches and 75 trades.

Official recognition of the contribution by women to the war effort came in 1946 when Parliament announced plans to retain women in the Armed Forces on a permanent basis. Three years later, on 1 February 1949, the WRAF was re-formed.

Today some 600 officers and 4800 airwomen serve in the Service and are employed in most ground branches and trade groups. Women enjoy equal rights in pay and employment with their male counterparts and are frequently found working alongside them in top positions of administration and engineering. They also compete on equal terms for promotion, appointments and training courses. Women are now permitted to fly most RAF aircraft types, with the exception of high-performance fighters and bombers.

In addition to serving in the UK, members of the WRAF are currently serving in Hong Kong, Cyprus, Gibraltar, Germany, Holland, Belgium, Ascension Island and the Falkland Islands; there is also one WRAF officer serving in America.

BASIC AIR COMBAT MANOEUVRES

Scissors

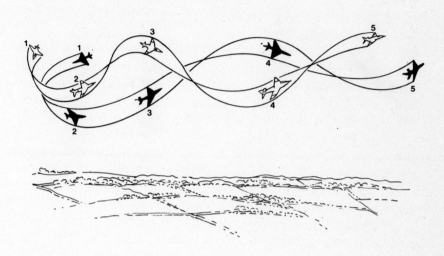

Rolling Scissors

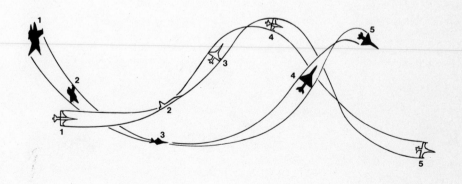

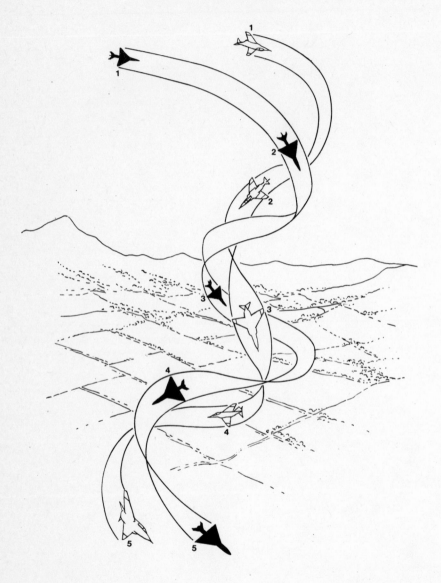

High-Speed Yo-Yo

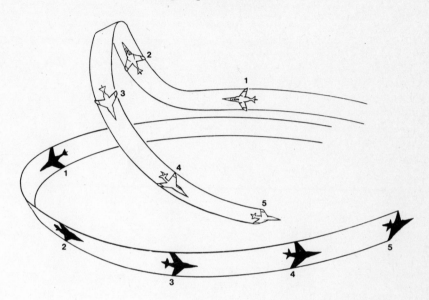

Low-Speed Yo-Yo

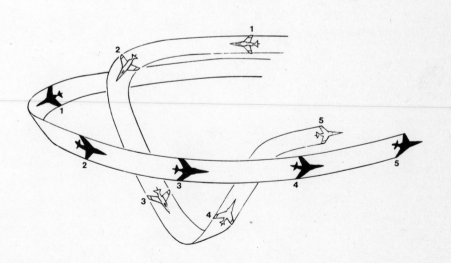

Lag-Pursuit Roll

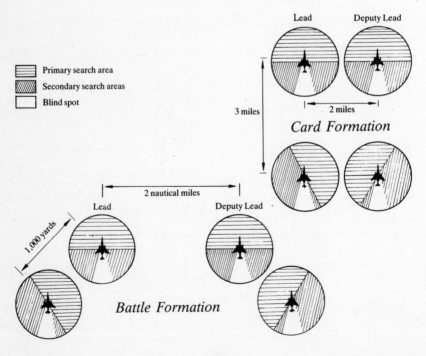

BASIC TACTICAL FORMATIONS

Primary search area
Secondary search areas
Blind spot

Lead   Deputy Lead

3 miles

2 miles

Card Formation

2 nautical miles

Lead   Deputy Lead

1,000 yards

Battle Formation

THE HARDENED AIRCRAFT SHELTER

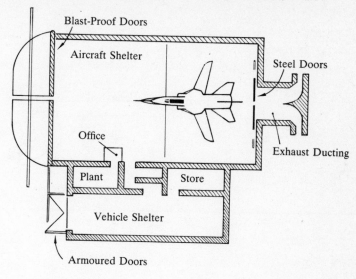

Blast-Proof Doors

Aircraft Shelter

Steel Doors

Office

Exhaust Ducting

Plant

Store

Vehicle Shelter

Armoured Doors

THE PILOT BRIEFING FACILITY

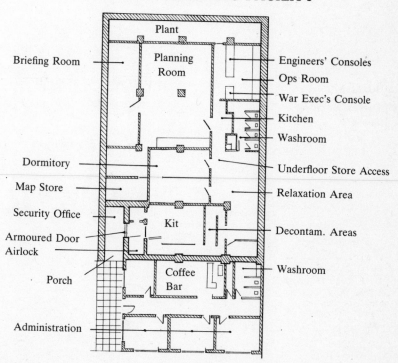

Plant

Planning Room

Briefing Room

Engineers' Consoles

Ops Room

War Exec's Console

Kitchen

Washroom

Dormitory

Underfloor Store Access

Map Store

Relaxation Area

Security Office

Kit

Armoured Door

Decontam. Areas

Airlock

Porch

Coffee Bar

Washroom

Administration

BUCCANEER PAVE SPIKE ATTACK PROFILE

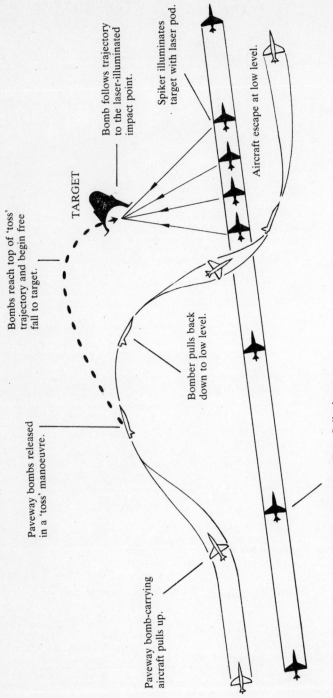

Bombs reach top of 'toss' trajectory and begin free fall to target.

Bomb follows trajectory to the laser-illuminated impact point.

Spiker illuminates target with laser pod.

TARGET

Aircraft escape at low level.

Paveway bombs released in a 'toss' manoeuvre.

Bomber pulls back down to low level.

Paveway bomb-carrying aircraft pulls up.

Aircraft carrying a Pave Spike laser designation pod runs in at low level. This aircraft is the 'Spiker'.

INDEX